The
Track

A Journey from Tragedy to Triumph

Jennifer Fox

ISBN 978-1-64300-104-3 (Paperback)
ISBN 978-1-64300-105-0 (Digital)

Covenant Books, Inc.
11661 Hwy 707
Murrells Inlet, SC 29576
www.covenantbooks.com

Photo: Holly Flood Shapiro

This book is dedicated to Gregory Allen Foster, Jr.
For "Brother"
Love,
"Sissy"

Contents

1

The Call

But now, O Jacob, listen to the Lord who created you. O Israel, the one who formed you says, "Do not be afraid, for I have ransomed you. I have called you by your name; you are mine."
—Isaiah 43:1 (NLT)

Who would be calling at this time of night? I thought. After all, it was an ordinary brisk spring that Thursday night in April of 1994. Cellular networks had started to emerge in the 1990s. However, common folk in rural upstate New York were not privy to much in terms of telecommunication systems beyond landline home telephones. Nonetheless, a cordless telephone device, which was popular at the time, was a technological upgrade from twenty years earlier when I was a little girl.

Back then in the "old days," as my kids commonly refer to the years when I was their age, my petite frame would have been frequently stationed on the *register*, which was what I called the heating vent positioned on the dining room floor of Grandma and Grandpa Daley's house. My two younger brothers and I often quarreled about whose turn it was to stand on the peculiarly popular rusty metal grid encased in the hardwood floors of our grandparents' one-hundred-year-old home on a farmland in the country. The furnace blower affixed to the wood stove in the cellar propelled hot air up through the warming aperture. As I took up residency on the register, the

7

warm ventilation wafted up my dress, causing the bottom of my skirt to puff out as I stood nearby my grandmother while she gossiped most of the morning on a party line, which was the communal four-party-telephone circuit neighbors shared back in my early childhood years. Each home was assigned a specific ring or sequence of rings that beckoned which residence was being summoned. One long ring and one short ring was the signal for my grandparents' telephone number. I recognized it well. We spent a considerable amount of time there growing up. Our family lived just down the road from Grandma and Grandpa Daley's house so the proximity was close enough to make daily visits. Moreover, the dysfunction and brokenness in my parents' marriage led to an assortment of bitter ingredients that created the ideal recipe for sudden middle-of-the-night relocations in and out of my mother's parents' residence.

On any given dawn, the aroma of homemade buttermilk pancakes filled the atmosphere as we awoke to Grandma spooning the batter onto a buttered cast-iron griddle over a gas stove burner. Beyond the scent of breakfast was the fragrance of Lavender Sachet fabric softener emanating from the washroom between the kitchen and bathroom. Grandma rose early and began her day's work, which increased on the mornings when their home had become our haven. A mother of eight and grandmother of twenty-five-plus grandchildren at that time, she was quite accustomed to serving her large family. She never complained and rather always seemed jovial, usually singing hymns as she waded through our clothing we had thrown in large black trash bags that accompanied us through the rotating front door of the back porch that led to their kitchen. Some mornings, we rose to the rickety sound of the pulley on the clothesline as Grandma hung our clothes out to dry and the familiar scent of lavender fabric softener in the country air. Often, the sound of the worn-out and overly used washing machine was muffled by the tone of Grandma's voice on the telephone. She loved to sit in the dining room and gossip on the phone for hours with her daughters, sisters, and sisters-in-law. I could almost smell the lavender sachet and buttermilk pancakes on the griddle as I recalled the sound of my grandmother's voice and chuckle on the telephone. A memory of a particular phone conversation comes to mind.

Grandma was on the phone with Aunt Edith. They were having a friendly visit. Fifteen minutes into their conversation, they heard a click, click sound. Ignoring the noise, they continued to talk about anything and everything. Twenty minutes went by, they heard it again. Click! Click! *Several minutes more passed when the neighbor Jack scolded the two women. "Get off the phone! You've been on it all morning!"*

> *Grandma was witty, and in her playful sense of humor, she quickly bellowed back, "Well, you ought to know. You've been listening in the whole time!"*
>
> Bang! *He slammed the receiver in their ears. Grandma and Aunt Edith chuckled and finished up their conversation to free up the party line for the neighbors.*

I am a firm believer that my grandparents were a means of God's grace and provision in our lives, yet even so, they couldn't protect us from … well, back to the late-night phone call in April 1994. Rare was the occasion that anyone called after nine o'clock in the evening in our hometown where crickets chirping was the only sound that could be heard off in the distance after dark. I called this quaint village and its rural surroundings home for most of my entire life. It was a small close-knit community in the Adirondack Mountains in bucolic Central New York, primarily made up of blue-collar workers who lived humble and simple lives. There wasn't very much that was newsworthy enough to call about past 9:00 p.m. After all, any big happenings on this native soil were typically after high school football games on Saturdays.

During football season, it was just commonplace on a Saturday afternoon for the entire municipality to appear reminiscent of Christmas morning. Sidewalks bordering local businesses were barren. The only road lined with incoming traffic was Slawson Street, which led to my *alma mater*, James A. Green High School. Some anxious spectators opted to walk the concrete path that led to DCS, home of the Dolgeville Central School's Blue Devils. Doing so allowed them to bypass the line of blue-and-white graffitied vehicles complete with streamers and balloons affixed to the antennas and bumpers of otherwise gridlocked commuters en route to the game. These local travelers didn't mind the one day of the week there would be any amount of traffic in this village that was so rural it lacked any traffic lights other than the yellow flashing light at the four-way stop located at the bottom of the school hill.

The sacrifice was worth the reward to these die-hard fans. Passengers lined up in their festive chariots and typically adorned themselves in blue-and-white Blue Devils athletic wear. There wasn't usually much question in an onlooker's gaze as to which football player any given enthusiastic supporter was there to cheer for. The jersey number of the player they were there to support was commonly painted on the face of the doting fan and any other visible flesh like temporary tattoos designed with paint. Once the procession of vehicles secured parking spots, masses of devoted enthusiasts gathered on the football field to applause and praise their hometown heroes. This was the high school football team that commonly took home championship titles. Away games didn't seem to change the outlook of the dedicated groupies. Regardless of distance, most townspeople thought nothing of following the team's school buses any amount of distance to other destinations where they would shout from the stands, "Go Big Blue!" In fact, it was common that the bleachers of committed fans dressed in blue and white, often outnumbered the home team's colors at away games. However, this was not a Saturday. It was not football season. In fact, it wasn't even a customary school day the following day. Friday was a scheduled day off for students at DCS. It was a designated superintendent's conference day, which gifted students with a three-day weekend. It had otherwise been a customary day up to this point.

I graduated from DCS four years earlier in June 1990. Following along in the footsteps of my peers, I left home shortly thereafter to attend college. However, I recently dropped out and relocated back to my hometown due to some extenuating circumstances. I became a single mother to my son Zachary as the result of a failed relationship that had begun many years prior in high school. Thus, a college degree became secondary, and survival became my primary goal at that time since I was my son's sole provider. I worked at the local hospital as a front desk switchboard operator and occasionally in the business office as needed. I drove my twenty-one-month-old son, the apple of my eye to day care that morning. I was blessed to have the wife of a local pastor take care of my son for me at a flat rate of sixty dollars per week, a budget rate that stretched my minimum-wage paycheck thin back then while I worked full time. It was a mandatory requirement of my position to work an occasional evening shift as well as alternating weekends.

My teenage brothers often babysat their nephew if my parents were unavailable during day care off hours. My two younger brothers lived in an upstairs apartment with our mom. They moved in with her after our parents divorced. We had an unusual bond as brothers and sister. I have seldom witnessed other sibling unions that resembled ours; perhaps it was the result of all we had been through together. Hardship and life trials have a way of bonding relationships securely. We had certainly experienced our fair share.

I left work earlier in the evening, picked up Zachary from day care, and traveled back to our modest apartment. I prepared his dinner, gave him a bath, read him a bedtime story, and tucked him into bed for the night at 8:00 p.m. My boyfriend of eight months, Harry, was coming over. We had plans to have a quiet and relaxing evening on the sofa. It was must-see TV night, and we had planned to watch all our favorite Thursday night primetime line-up. *Friends* was my favorite, however, I was equally a fan of *ER*. Since Zachary was down for the night, I changed into something cozy. Harry arrived and we just settled in on the sofa when the phone rang. It wasn't all that far from the living room to the kitchen where the phone was ringing, yet it was so arduous to drag myself from the couch I comfortably nestled into, dozing off next to my love after a long day. Although it was tempting to continue resting my eyes that had grown so heavy, it was peculiar that the telephone was ringing so late at night. I thought that it was likely a prank call. Those were popular back then. Having just had phone service connected in my new apartment days prior to without an answering machine yet, whoever was calling was persistent as the phone continued ringing and ringing. I finally gave into the relentless interruption to my relaxation and dragged my sluggish body to the kitchen.

"Hello?" I paused to listen. "What? I don't understand. Where is he? Is he okay? We're on our way!" Harry knew from the tone of my voice and the obvious change in countenance on my face that this was no social call. He pursued me in the kitchen. Distraught and confused, I relayed, "It's my brother. There's been some sort of accident. I don't know all the details, but we need to get to the hospital right away!"

We scrambled, panicked and frazzled. I ran upstairs to where my son was sleeping soundly and lifted him out of his crib. With little time to prepare to go out with a baby, I wrapped him in a blanket and grabbed a spare diaper as Harry filled a bottle with milk downstairs. We rushed out the door to the parking lot where my little black Grand Am was parked. I hurriedly strapped Zachary securely into his car seat. With Harry behind the wheel, we frantically sped out of the bay. We proceeded down the steep hill from the apartment complex, traveled along Main Street through town, and made our way to route 5, the highway that led to the local hospital and also my place of employment where I had been instructed to go. About halfway to the hospital as we neared the swanky and popular restaurant Beardslee Castle, we noticed emergency vehicle lights in the distance. As we crossed over the Montgomery County Bridge, a bridge spanning over the East Canada Creek and lined by train tracks, an ambulance pulled out of an access road just ahead of us.

Unaware of the location of the accident my brother had been involved in, I asked Harry, "I wonder if that is the scene of the accident I was just called about or something else is going on." We followed the ambulance from route 5 all the way to the hospital. Something just didn't seem right. I had a very uneasy feeling in the pit of my stomach. "Why is that ambulance not traveling very fast, and why are there no emergency lights flashing or sirens sounding?" I inquired of Harry, not that he would have had any further answers than I did. I was likely looking for some assurance that everything was going to be okay. Intuitively, I think I knew somewhere deep within myself that everything was not all right. One thing was for sure, it was by far the longest fifteen-minute ride down a well-traveled road that I had ever taken.

The red emergency room sign could finally be seen in the distance. We were getting close. The ambulance made a left-hand turn toward the emergency department. However, in keeping with a sequence of unusual events, not only did the ambulance not signal any flashing lights or sound a siren, but for some strange reason, it wasn't pulling up in front of the main entrance doors to the emergency department as it normally did. But this was not a normal set of circumstances. Instead, it continued around to the back of the hospital. Since this hospital was also my place of employment, I was familiar with locations, procedures, and policies. Why was the ambulance going around to the rear of the hospital building? I hadn't seen that before. The only department of the infirmary I was aware of that was located in the back of the small medical facility was the morgue, which absolutely ruled out any possibility that this particular ambulance was remotely connected to the accident my brother was involved in. After all, those types of circumstances only happened in other people's lives. Surely that would have nothing to do with my specific set of circumstances in being called out this particular night. Clearly there was a more logical explanation.

Harry parked the car in the hospital parking lot, and I ran ahead, across the street and up the hill to the entrance of the emergency room doors. Although I had no real picture in my mind of what to expect when I arrived, where to report to or who would be there, I did not prepare for the scene that was unfolding that I would bear witness to. It was mass chaos. It was as if I was looking through the lens of a camera that was not entirely in focus as the images ahead were blurred and seemed to play out in slow motion. *Who are these people, and why are they all here? Okay, there's my dad. Finally, a familiar face. He doesn't look well. Wait, there's my aunt and uncle next to him. Why are they here at the hospital at this hour?* My mind was spinning in confusion. I started to run toward my father for answers.

As I did, I noticed a woman lying in the street in front of the emergency room main entrance. She was screaming with such a horrifying, deep screech, I can almost hear it echo in my head. There were people gathered all around her. As the crowd around her repositioned themselves, I caught a glimpse of the woman.

"Mom!" I screamed as I ran to my mother's side. "Mom, what is going on?" I couldn't quite make sense of what she was saying or talking about.

She kept repeating, "He wanted eggs! He wanted me to make him eggs!" as she wept, screamed, and moaned in agony. Everyone was embracing and crying, it didn't make sense.

"He's gonna be okay, right? How badly is he injured? He has a broken leg but he's gonna be all right! They told me on the phone that he only had a broken leg!" Starting to put the pieces of a very messy picture together, I began frantically interrogating everyone within ear shot. "Why are you all looking at me like that? Why won't anyone answer me?" I shouted at the crowd of familiar faces I had begun to recognize as various family members.

As confusion and panic waged war on my mind, it felt as if the earth around me was spinning. A dark sadness and pain so deep it cut like a knife, draped itself around me like an invisible yet tangible heavy force. The weight of an incredible presence of darkness pulled my shoulders down and pushed my entire being forward as I doubled over in despair. Like waves crashing against me in a category four hurricane, I couldn't see clearly through the oceans of tears that gushed from my eyes. I placed my hands firmly against either side of the temples on my head as the force of great sorrow and writhing pain caused the earth around me to gyrate and the ground beneath me crumble. It was like I was looking at a scene all around me through shattered glass as my eyes were trying to focus like the lens of a camera, alternating from blurriness to sharpness.

As this storm raged all around me, I caught a glimpse of my little brother. He was a child and the absolutely cutest Irish-looking little boy with strawberry blonde hair, hazel eyes, and freckles. He was running toward me, smiling and laughing. He seemed so happy. The sun shone behind his head. After running through the lush green grass of a field covered with white dandelions, he stopped, bent down, and picked one of the white cotton ball flowers. As he continued running with his freshly picked flower clasped in his tiny little hand, the air around him was filled with the fluffy residue blowing off the little weed. Our mother would put his gift in a water-filled vase she collected our blossoms in and displayed it in the kitchen window above the sink where she washed dishes with lemon-scented Joy. He enjoyed bringing flowers to our mom. Sometimes they would both end up with a case of poison ivy as a result, but neither one minded. It wasn't an important element in the trail he blazed through the green field, covered in fluffy white dandelion seeds dispersed and scattered on the earth as he made his mark on the world.

2

A Soul Is Born

Before I formed you in the womb I knew you.
—Jeremiah 1:5 (NKJV)

"It's time," my mom Judy announced to my dad Greg who was sleeping soundly. He returned home from an exhausting twelve-hour day at work not long before the big announcement. She had just finished putting groceries away and tucking me, aged two and a half years old, into bed for the night. It was 1975.

Dad was deployed due to the ongoing effects of the Vietnam War much of the time from 1972 (when I was born) until 1975 when our little family grew from three to four. Where Dad was exactly during those times of deployment, no one except him and those who were privy to classified information knew back then. The missions were so top secret that letters home to Mom and me, even to his mother, were frozen coming and going so that the location of military operations would not be revealed to anyone outside of the mission via postmark on an envelope. The days were long and lonely for an air force wife back then. Mom and Dad had been high school sweethearts since age fourteen and married after graduation in 1971. There was a lottery and draft system in effect for the United States military back in the early seventies during the Vietnam War era. Aware that his number was due to come up in the lottery, Dad enlisted in the United States Air Force rather than the alternative, which was being drafted. Knowing a future career in the military was probable, voluntarily enlisting rather than being drafted allowed him the opportunity to choose the same branch of service as his eldest brother who was also likely to be drafted. There was chatter surrounding the circumstances to place one of the two brothers in the marines and the other in the army. So to secure the possibility of staying together, the two joined the air force. Although they were sent through basic training and some other various training together, the pair was eventually separated when Uncle George was stationed in Dover, Delaware, and Dad and his new bride were stationed in Plattsburgh, New York.

Plattsburgh, nicknamed the Lake City or the Burgh, was located in the North Country region on the western shore of Lake Champlain in the northeastern part of the state of New York on the Canadian border. Plattsburgh Air Force Base (PAFB) was a vibrant and notable military base, serving as the location of the Strategic Air Command's primary wing on the East Coast due to its geographic desirability. The base's location in Champlain Valley, protected by the shadow of the Adirondack Mountains, ensured consistent and year-round weather that was safe for takeoffs and landings. The 380th Bombardment, Aerospace, and Refueling wings stationed at PAFB included B-52 bombers and air-refueling tankers. It made Plattsburgh a vibrant military city. In 1975, the population in Plattsburgh was about 20,000 people.

Mom was a young newlywed wife. She was about a three-hour drive from her family and the only place she had ever called home while her husband was away 268 out of 365 days a year in the few years following their marriage. Dad spent his air force days on a KC-135Q tanker, refueling SR-71 Blackbirds in Vietnam and surrounding regions midair as the enemy made it their mission to shoot them down. Disabling the tankers responsible for refueling the U.S. fighter jets would "kill two birds with one stone," as they say, thus making him and his colleagues a desirable target from enemy lines. Mom spent her days in military housing, taking care of me with little support from her family due to the distance between them. She worked part-time at Noah's Ark, the local pet shop, to give her some sense of socialization and additional income. She eventually met another military family on base, the Hoags. Jo Hoag's husband John was also deployed due to the war. She became a treasured friend to Mom and babysat for me when Mom worked. Jo's son JJ and I became friends and playmates. We were around the same age.

In God's kindness, Mom and Dad were united in the same location on February 7, 1975. It was a usual day in the life of our small military family. Dad worked all day that day, doing repairs on the KC-135A plane as the assistant crew chief. Mom, nine months pregnant, went grocery shopping that Friday evening at a local supermarket when she began feeling a lot of pressure. She was scheduled for a routine C-section the following week on Valentine's Day. Due to some complications during childbirth two and a half years prior when giving birth to me, a C-section had become medically necessary for subsequent deliveries back then. The maternity hospital bag was packed and ready to go since they already had several trial runs due to false labor. It was a cold night, and although snow had accumulated on the ground throughout the winter months, snow was not falling that particular night, which was unusual in the north.

Mom and Dad made their way to Champlain Valley Hospital, a civilian hospital, since the military base hospital was no longer delivering babies. It worked out just as well since this civilian hospital only charged military families $25 back then for a baby delivery. Times sure have changed since then. Currently in 2017, it costs families about $25,000 for a brief stay in the swanky labor and delivery departments of modern, nonmilitary hospital facilities. Nonetheless, even back in 1975, $25 was a bargain for the return. The soon-to-be-parents of two called on their faithful military friend and neighbor Jo Hoag to care for me as they made their way to the hospital. Mom was experiencing full-blown symptoms of labor. As childbirth was clearly impending, the medical staff took her back to the operating room for a C-section.

"It's a boy!" the doctor announced as he placed the six-pound, eight-ounce, and twenty-one-inch-long infant in his mother's arms.

The young mother was emotional and overcome with great pride and joy as she gazed into her son's sad-shaped eyes framed with red eyebrows. The infant's innocence was pure and precious as his tiny fingers grasped his mother's finger. He puckered and smacked his narrow lips, as he rooted looking for a place to nurse. Once the final sutures in her womb were secured, she was transferred to the recovery room. Her husband was greeted in a nearby waiting room, anticipating a birth announcement, when attending medical personnel approached him and asked, "Mr. Foster, would you like to join your wife and meet your son?"

"A son? I have a son?" He almost couldn't believe the news he secretly hoped to hear. Although their daughter was very much wanted and loved, having a son in that time period in their close-knit, all-American families, was a status symbol of pride. A son would pass along the torch to carry on the family name. The proud new father entered the recovery room to be reunited with his wife and meet for the first time, his namesake, Gregory Allen Foster Jr.

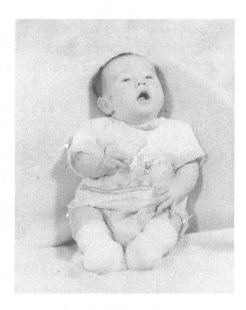

Mom's parents traveled from back home to Plattsburgh to meet their new grandchild and assist their daughter post C-section, which was considered major surgery back in those days. In addition to meeting their new grandson and being present for their daughter, Grandma and Grandpa Daley also helped care for me while my parents and new sibling stayed at the hospital. I was ecstatic to be a new big sister of a baby brother.

About a week post-op, Dad and I pulled up outside of the hospital in our baby blue 1966 Ford Fairlane 500 to pick up Mom and my new baby brother and escort them both back home. Use of a car seat back in 1975 was not a legal mandate. Mom held Greg Jr., whom I had already nicknamed "Brother," on her lap in the front passenger seat, and I took over a newfound position standing on the middle of the front bench seat between my parents. Our family of four traveled up the Northway, a major highway that ran through the North Country, with music from the Beach Boys, Chicago, and Frankie Valli and the Four Seasons playing on the eight-track tape player.

The first few weeks at home with a newborn and toddler were not easy. Grandma and Grandpa Daley had to return to their little hometown and brother was a colicky baby. He cried a lot, wanted to eat every two hours, and didn't require as much sleep as our exhausted mother did. To complicate matters further, Mom acquired a bad case of influenza. Her abdomen incision became infected, and due to the excessive coughing from the flu, her sutures tore. The pain was so intense that the thought of seeking treatment from her doctor who would need to touch the area was more pain than she desired to endure. So she did what any other young, desperate mother would do. She phoned home to her mother. Grandma Daley expressed her concern for her daughter's health, however, with knowledge that her daughter was not going to seek medical care, she advised her to treat the infected incision with hydrogen peroxide, antibiotic ointment, and over-the-counter butterfly stitches, an adhesive shaped like a butterfly that could be used to draw the incision together. The flu ran its viral course, and the infection eventually cleared. The incision healed but it left obvious scarring.

Brother continued to require little sleep, getting up like clockwork every two hours for a bottle of formula. Our sleep-deprived mother would inquire of other mothers within her inner circle regarding the age that their babies started sleeping through the night in hopes that someone would answer with a relatable similar struggle. However, despite reports of babies elsewhere sleeping through the night by age 3–6 months, the pattern of sleepless nights continued for Mom and Brother until he was nearly three years old—at least, that's how she remembers it.

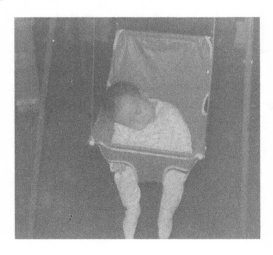

Nonetheless, Brother and I were the absolute apples of her eyes, and there was nothing she desired more on earth than to be our mother. Dad was deployed again just a few months after Brother's birth. With Dad continually away from home, the separation took a toll on my parents' marriage and our family. To complicate marital issues further, Dad's predisposition to alcoholism began rearing its head in an environment where Friday Beer Bash among air force peers became tradition. Additionally, his unit often stayed in jungles where malaria was prominent. As a result, there was concern about drinking the water there. As an alternative, his troop stayed hydrated on beer and Jack Daniels. The daily intake of alcohol as a substitute for water combined with the effects of other factors which negatively impacted the mental and emotional health of military personnel, created a cosmic collision where genetics already played a strong role.

Mom didn't return to work at the pet store. Instead, she spent her days changing diapers, caring for two small children, and folding laundry. Often, she folded the laundry and placed it in baskets to transport upstairs to the second floor of our apartment during the rare occasion that she was most likely to have both hands and a hip free of children during naptime. In the meantime, Brother, who had eventually become mobile as he crawled around the parameter of the military base housing unit, often found entertainment in taking his mother's hard work out of laundry baskets and tossing it down the flight of stairs. It was difficult for Mother to become angry with him. After all, he had naturally sad, hazel-colored eyes framed with auburn eyebrows and finely textured hair that often wouldn't lay flat. His narrow lips opened when he giggled, flashing his little white buck teeth as Mom attempted the impossible – scolding him.

Although our family was separated often and things were frequently difficult for us, there were many things about our life in Plattsburgh during those first few years of my life that were memorable. We lived across the street from the Plattsburgh International Raceway where we sometimes attended NASCAR races. Brother and I laughed and giggled every time the sound of a race car zoomed by.

Santa's Workshop also wasn't a far drive away, and we enjoyed visiting the attraction where all things made it feel like Christmas year-round. One of our favorite stops was a local Dairy Queen. It was a treat to go there for an occasional ice cream cone, which reminded us of the local ice cream shop back home in our hometown.

MILES
TO
NORTH POLE

Nonetheless, all good, and I might add, not-so-good things eventually come to an end. Thus, our three-to-four year status of being stationed at PAFB concluded. Our little family of four, from nearly the furthest northeastern point of the United States on the globe all the way to the border of Canada, pursued a journey of drastic changes. We were transferred to an air force military base bordering Mexico, Carswell Air Force Base in Fort Worth, Texas.

3

Brother's Keeper

Love one another with brotherly affection.
—Romans 12:10 (ESV)

The journey rarely is perfect in this thing called life. As circumstances would have it, our young military family of four said good-bye to the place we had called home for about four years and made our long, twenty-four-hour journey from Plattsburgh, New York, to Carswell Air Force Base in Fort Worth, Texas. It was May 1976. Although it was nearing the end of spring and the beginning of summer was quickly approaching the following month, it was cold when we pulled out of our driveway one last time in that old 1972 Mercury Cougar.

Speaking of the Mercury Cougar, Mom's father, Grandpa Daley never liked or approved of that car much. You see, Grandpa Daley was a simple man. He was a dairy farmer as his chosen profession after returning from WWII as a soldier in the United States Army from 1942–1945. Actually, he pursued logging as his source of providing for his family upon completion of his military career. However, he eventually became a dairy farmer. Grandpa Daley was especially close with God and very wise when it came to things pertaining to his relationship with the Almighty. In fact, it was in the barn where he first encountered his heavenly Father. Grandpa said that's where he was saved. He often told the story of the day he was in the old faded and weathered wooden barn behind their white house in rural Central New York in a little town called Salisbury Center. He was milking cows and listening to an evangelist on the radio when he heard angels singing the most beautiful music he had ever heard. The angelic sounds were so powerful that he fell to his knees right there on the hay-covered barn floor and prayed, asking God to save him. He served the Lord for forty years after that encounter. He lived a humble, quiet life and believed that others would be prudent to glean from his example. To him, our gold Mercury Cougar was a luxury car. It used a lot of gas. That mere fact by itself was a factor he took into consideration as he chalked the vehicle up to being extravagant. After all, there had just been an energy crisis in the entire United States.

In October 1973, the members of Organization of Arab Petroleum Exporting Countries (or OAPEC) proclaimed an oil embargo in response to the States' decision to resupply the Israeli military during the Yom Kippur War, which lasted until March 1974. However, fuel shortages and sky-high prices continued throughout much of the decade. There was a gasoline mandate in effect that citizens could only go to the gas pump to refuel on various structured even and odd days. It certainly wasn't the best timing to own a "luxury" car that was also a gas hog. Nonetheless, the cross-country journey from New York to Texas was going to be long (and require quite a bit of gas) so we had better get moving along.

We made our journey southwest. Mom couldn't help but notice how green Mother Nature appeared to be in southern states like

Tennessee. As we crossed through an impoverished neighborhood in Arkansas, Mom noticed little children running around barefoot and half naked outside rundown houses with broken windows. It hurt her heart to see such poverty in America. She hadn't traveled much in her twenty-three years on earth and had never seen many other parts of the world. She was raised in a small town in upstate New York on a farm in the country and rarely traveled. She had barely adjusted to living a few hours north in the same state as her family. As she pondered out the window, her stomach felt queasy, becoming emotional with the reality that she was indeed a long way from home. She became homesick and missed her folks. When we finally arrived at our destination, it was hot, especially since we left New York in warm winter clothing. It didn't take long for our young family to stare the reality of cultural differences in the face that we were indeed not in Kansas anymore and that this was not the north or even the east coast, for that matter. We were a long way from home and family, the weather was different, the southern accent was far different than our northern accent, the culture was different, and the time zone was different. Although we were reluctantly excited about a fresh start, we were also very much aware that it would take time to adjust.

We stayed in a hotel while we awaited final arrangements to close on our new home and for our furniture and belongings to arrive from Plattsburgh in a military moving truck. After two weeks of hotel living with two small children ages three and one and a half year old and a small accident when Brother fell off one of the hotel beds from using it as a trampoline, Mom and Dad approached Mickey, the man they were purchasing our new home from. He allowed us to move into the home while we awaited formal closing procedures. Mickey had just gone through a divorce and gave Mom and Dad one condition in order to move into the home early—allow his dog to stay at the home until he could make other arrangements for it at his mother's home where he was temporarily staying. He assured them that the dog had been raised with his children and was friendly. Of course, the couple agreed to the terms of the arrangement and prepared to move into their new home. A couple of days later, our moving truck arrived. We finally had our furniture and personal belongings to begin furnishing our new, little, green, ranch-style home and making it our own. We each went to work, unpacking and putting things in order. There was a swing set and sandbox in the backyard. So I pleaded my case with Mom and Dad to allow my little brother and I to go to the backyard and play. Our parents gave us permission. After all, it was a win-win for everyone involved. Brother and I would entertain ourselves outside since our toys were still packed and the bedrooms were in disarray, leaving Mom and Dad to unpack free of interruptions and distractions.

It was a hot, sunny day in White Settlement, Texas, a suburb of Fort Worth. Brother and I were happily playing in the backyard while Mom supervised us from a nearby kitchen window above the sink, which directly overlooked the backyard. We played while she unpacked boxes of dishes, placing each cup and plate in the wooden cabinets. Brother and I were running around excitedly in our new yard, laughing and chasing one another. After all, this was unchartered territory for us. Up to this point, we had lived in air force base housing where a large backyard was not something we were familiar with.

With a dish towel in hand, Mom busily went about her work when she suddenly heard an ear-piercing scream at the door. She frantically dashed to the door to find me standing there bleeding from my face and neck and crying for help. Mom panicked at the sight of her petite three-year-old daughter standing before her covered in blood. She quickly took the dish towel in her hand and wrapped it around my tiny neck where my large jugular vein protruded, squirting blood with every pump of my racing heartbeat.

Dad heard the high-pitched shrieking of his wife and daughter and ran inside the house. In shock, he tore open boxes labeled bathroom, pulled towels out, and began wrapping the linens around his young daughter's neck in a desperate attempt to stop the massive amount of blood loss. As he wrung blood from saturated towels and reapplied them to his daughter's mangled face and neck, Mom ran outside and scurried my brother Greg Jr. into the house. They loaded their children into the car and sped out of the driveway in search of the closest hospital in their new surroundings. They followed blue signs with a large H and tuned in to the CB radio in their vehicle for assistance from emergency officials. Meanwhile, I was losing a lot of blood rapidly. Mom and Dad were nearly out of their minds in terror. They feared that their precious daughter would bleed to death. With emergency flashers going off from all four corners of the gold Mercury, they exceeded the speed limit with help from emergency officials on the CB radio and likely a little help from the good Lord above. Their mission was clear, and planning the funeral of their three-year-old daughter was not an option they were willing to accept.

Greg Jr., only fifteen months old at the time, expressed deep concern for his big sister he referred to as "Sissy." I was his absolute best friend in the world, his playmate, and his protector. From the moment he was born into our family, Brother had been the apple of my blue-green eyes. He had essentially become a real-life baby doll to me. I mothered and nurtured him as if he was my own child. That's just the type of bond we had. It was unique and special. In fact, it was precisely my mothering that caused the life-threatening crisis right in that very moment. But there I go again, putting the cart in front of the horse.

Finally by the grace and guidance of Almighty God Himself, the blue signs bearing the H symbol led us to our intended destination. We followed the red signs to the emergency department. Dad parked the car, ran to the passenger door, took me from mother's arms, and instructed her to grab Brother from the back seat. They ran from the car to the entrance doors. Like a lifeless ragdoll, flopping with every stride Dad took as he ran, I continued screaming in and out of consciousness in fear, pain, and shock as my undersized body continued losing blood. Dad flung the doors of the emergency department wide open as he cradled me in his arms. Mom followed behind, carrying my brother as they desperately sought urgent medical treatment for their daughter. "My daughter has been attacked by a dog!" Dad bellowed, almost out of breath, to the desk clerk.

As other nearby medical personnel overheard the commotion, a team of doctors and nurses quickly responded to the crisis. As emergency personnel took me from my father's arms and carried me back to the trauma department where life-saving measures would begin, Mom became faint. It was unbearable for her to witness the horrifying scene, and massive amounts of blood spurting from her beloved daughter's face and neck as her flesh was mangled in appearance. The sound of my screaming and crying was more than she could bear. As she became keenly aware that she indeed was absolutely going to pass out, the nurses helped her sit in the designated waiting area while dad followed behind the ER physician.

Brother was unable to speak very well but he could utter a few distinct words. Somehow he communicated his concern for me as he cried and begged to go back to the trauma room with Daddy and Sissy. Dad stopped and took hold of his son. "You need to help Mommy. She needs you."

"I need to go with Sissy. Sissy needs me." Brother was scared, confused, and sad about what happened to Sissy, however, he obeyed his father and stayed with his mom.

I was placed on a gurney and secured in place with straps to keep me as immobile as possible. Surrounded by a team of trauma military medical professionals, Dad stayed at my side throughout the three-hour process of suturing and life-saving measures. Nearly a hundred Novocain injections were administered throughout the process in an effort to numb the area, however, the injuries involved the muscle tissue so deeply that it was nearly impossible to completely desensitize the intense pain. I continued screaming so hysterically that I was given a sedative, but it merely took the edge off. The pain was too intense, the blood loss too great, and the shock and fear were far too overwhelming. No doubt the Almighty was giving our entire family strength in our time of need. There's really no other reasonable or logical explanation for getting through the unfathomable. Grandpa Daley always told us that God promised never to leave or forsake us. That theory would eventually be tested. We weren't necessarily religious people—at least, not yet.

The last suture was stitched carefully in place by the military captain and doctor. He was meticulous in his craft. He removed his gloves, washed his hands, and proceeded to the waiting room where my mother anxiously waited, hoping for some good news. "Your daughter is going to be just fine, Mrs. Foster," the doctor reported as he sighed in relief himself. It had been an intense few hours, and he bore a great burden upon his broad shoulders. "She required a lot of stitches, fifty-four to be exact. Fifty-four very tiny stitches so that the scar will be less noticeable."

Mom let out a visible sigh of relief and cried tears of joy at the news that I was going to be okay. She knew that there was a long road ahead. However, the most important matter at hand was that I had survived a terrible accident. It wasn't my predetermined time. My life had been spared.

It was a surreal moment as Mom and Dad returned home. They were grateful, in fact, that they were returning home with their daughter alive having been spared a tragedy, yet haunted by the memories they faced, revisiting the scene of events from earlier that day. Mom and Dad had placed a call to Mickey while they were still at the hospital. He was the previous owner of the home and the dog that attacked me. It was still unclear at that point with brother as the only eye witness to the dog attack. He was only fifteen months old and unable to communicate the details of the incident. One thing was for certain, they wanted the dog removed and needed to verify details, such as immunization records and the history of the canine. The dog had been removed from the property by the time the family returned home and was placed in quarantine for the mandated time period required by law after a dog bite incident. Mickey pleaded with the couple not to force him to euthanize the dog. He explained that the family pet was normally friendly and had been raised with his children who were already amid great loss due to a very messy divorce. Mom and Dad reluctantly agreed.

The days and weeks that followed were extremely difficult. I was in an excruciating amount of pain. Because my injuries involved predominantly my jaw, face, and neck, basic daily living tasks such as chewing food, drinking water, dressing, and bathing were especially grueling. When I was eventually able to speak about the details, I reported to my parents the sequence of events the best I could from the perspective of a three-year-old child. I explained that brother was playing with the dog's food and water bowls. "The dog was growling at Brother so I pushed him out of the way. Then the dog attacked me. That dog was on top of me under that big tree in the backyard, and he was biting my face. Then I got away from him and ran to the house," I told my parents.

The explanation seemed to be an accurate calculation of what had transpired that near tragic day. After all, I was my brother's keeper. That's what I always did from the day Mom and Dad brought my baby brother home from the hospital. I nurtured, mothered, protected, and kept him. This unfortunate event was nothing out of the ordinary. Meaning, that it's just what I did as my brother's Sissy. I protected and watched over him until I couldn't. Ironically, as the shoe was on the other foot, so to speak, my brother stayed by my side day after day, doing what I usually did. He helped me, nurtured me, and protected me. It was his turn to pay it forward. Although he was only fifteen months old, he understood enough to know that he was concerned for the sister he cared so much about. It was evident in the manner that he compassionately nursed me back to health and life.

Although our parents regretted the terrible accident that nearly cost them their daughter, they could somehow in the midst of great remorse find a slight sense of gratitude. After all, had I not been my brother's keeper on that day, the dog may have attacked him instead. If that had been the case, the consequences could have absolutely been a greater price to pay. He was only a baby, too small to sustain the type of attack, injuries, and blood loss that nearly claimed my life, even though I was only two and a half years older. Maybe for a minute, they caught a glimpse of God Almighty's sovereign hand of protection. Well, maybe they didn't recognize it or couldn't exactly identify it as such back then, but I'm sure they do now over forty years later. They faithfully reminded and praised me for my heroic protection of Brother on that day. *Should haves, could haves*, and *would haves* never really have benefitted anyone much other than in living condemned. Eventually, I healed and returned to normal with mothering, nurturing, playing with, loving, and being brother's keeper. I hoped it would always be that way until it wasn't.

4

And Then There Were Three

For where two or three gather in my name, there am I with them.
— Matthew 18:20 (NIV)

W ell, life goes on, so they say. There were a few hard weeks after the dog bite. Brother continued to help Mom and Dad with my care. In fact, he didn't really leave my side much until I was up and back to normal. Before long, the two of us were back outside in our new backyard, minus the dog as a third wheel. Our parents kept their word not to euthanize the dog. Mickey the dog owner moved on with his own personal legal troubles, and our family finally closed on our first home. It sure would be ideal to document that life was easy after so much hardship, but that wasn't the case. Sure, there were happy times, but unfortunately for our very young just-starting-out military family, the troublesome days outweighed the days when the sun would occasionally peek through the clouds.

As I just briefly mentioned a couple of chapters ago, Dad, only twenty-three years young at the time, began drinking quite heavily. His family genetics certainly didn't set him up for success. His father was an alcoholic, and there was a long history of relatives within his family who battled the bottle. As if family history and genetics were not enough to predispose him to trouble with alcohol, he learned at a very young age to self-medicate with liquor and beer. After all, he suffered the traumatizing effects of emotional and physical abuse of his mother, himself, and siblings at the hands of his father. He left home, family, and all that went along with it at age eighteen when he graduated from high school and enlisted in the military. He married my mom, his high school sweetheart, and took her on the journey to military life alongside him. She was as equally hopeful as he was that a removal from his toxic environment would solve all alcohol-related problems big and small. However, that wasn't the case. In fact, for all intents and purposes, I'd venture to say that back in the seventies, military enlistment came with certain expectations. Drinking was one of such expectations.

It was the Vietnam War era, and there was a mind-set amongst military soldiers that binge drinking was just par for the course. In fact, the more alcohol a soldier could tolerate, the more the "coolness" barometer would increase. It's just what they did. It's how they related and socialized. It's how they calculated one another's manhood and toughness. Every Friday was considered Friday Beer Bash. All the troops on the base would gather at various local establishments for a night of drinking (lots of it), fraternizing, playing darts and pool, women, and having fun. Of course, frequent deployments and missions supported excessive drinking. The mental, emotional, and physical effects of the war and all that these soldiers witnessed and participated in, which they had to keep confidential as most matters involving Vietnam were classified, created the perfect storm as they numbed and released the pain and negative psychological effects with a buzz. To complicate matters even further, when troops set up camp in the jungles of Vietnam, they were not only discouraged from drinking the malaria-infested water officially, they were unofficially encouraged to stay hydrated with beer and Jack Daniels as the alternative.

The genetic predisposition, abuse at home, military conditions, and effects of the war provided the perfect cocktail for a nineteen to twenty-three-year-old young adult to develop a pretty serious battle with alcoholism. No doubt, Dad's struggle with alcohol, coupled with constantly being separated from his family, was taking its toll on the newlyweds and young parents of small children. In fact, it's essentially what led us to our new home across the country, away from our support system. Dad eventually returned to Plattsburgh Air Force Base after the war had officially come to an end. It had officially come to an end several years prior according to public news media accounts, however, it was still very much ongoing unofficially and classified. After getting into some trouble and fights, Dad was sent to rehab in Ohio. When he returned, he and his military commander mutually agreed that it was in everyone's best interests for him to transfer to Carswell AFB in Fort Worth, Texas.

As the circle of life would have it, sometimes fleeing from the perceived source of trouble is enough to resolve problems and sometimes, it's just ... well, fleeing. Somehow these things have a way of following us around wherever we go. It begs the question that maybe outside circumstances, genetics and wars within aren't the problem, nor is self-medication, change of environment, or behavior modification an effective solution. Perhaps there's more to our complex makeup and design. If we truly are created in our mother's wombs and formed in God Almighty's image, just as Grandpa Daley told us was the case, then maybe, just maybe there's an inner void longing to be fulfilled. What if that void, which causes a war within the depths of our souls, craves a relationship with something or someone so much greater that we spend the entire span of our lives in search of supplemental nourishment for that which can never be satisfied with earthly things of this world? I hope to find the answers to those questions as we unpack this story together, you and me. So shall we?

Our family was transferred from the northeast to the southwest. The change in circumstances and environment were supposed to rectify all that had gone array in life, but somehow the earth still rotated and revolved around the sun in its orbit, the force of gravity still utilized the law of physics, and the troubles of life in a fallen world continued. Just as the sands of time sifted through the hour glass of life and the world turned, so did the young husband, father, and air force crew chief's drinking. He couldn't stop. He wanted to. He hated it yet loved it at the same time. The cosmic battle between love and hate and the guilt of his circumstances, caused him to drink more and placed his inner desires, cravings, and conscience at war with one another deep within his weary soul. The greater the guilt and shame, the more he self-medicated; the more he self-medicated, the more guilt and shame piled up, making him consume more Jack Daniels. It was a vicious cycle. He couldn't break free of addiction's curse and grip on his life or adequately be the husband and father he wanted to be.

A young, weary bride at her wit's end with her husband's drinking and all the consequences that followed closely behind, discouraged by broken promises and lack of peace and hope, packed up with my brother and me, and left Dad. She found solace back home with her family in Upstate New York. The loss of his family should have been a wake-up call for Dad. It was, yet it wasn't enough to make him stop. In fact, drowning deeper in guilt, shame, and convictions of failure, he spiraled further out of control as alcohol dominated his life. As if the complicated variables weren't difficult enough for our struggling family, Mom and Dad learned they were expecting their third child. A child is always a gift of God. However, it was undeniable that the timing wasn't exceptional. Nonetheless, Almighty God had His way. Then again, He really doesn't ever *not* get His way. After all, He *is* in control of the entire universe. Some believe that inexplicable mystery. Some can't wrap their feeble and flawed human minds around the anonymities of God. Regardless, believing something or not doesn't negate the facts and realities of timeless truths. It was God's plan all along that despite all their troubles, Mom and Dad were always meant to bring this child into the world.

As fate would have it, Mom and Dad welcomed their third and final child into the world on September 7, 1977 in Fort Worth, Texas. He was given the name of both of his grandfathers combined. Well, if you ask Mom today, she will tell you that her youngest was named solely after her father, William Edward Daley, who was given the name James George Daley at birth. How that happened, well, that's another story for another time. But if you ask dad, whose father's name was George Edgar Foster Jr., he will tell you his third child's name is the birth name of his maternal grandfather James and his paternal grandfather George. Either way, no matter which grandfather was represented, two became three, and our family of four became a family of five. James George Foster, nicknamed Jimmy, joined our family.

5

Adam, Eve, and a Little Bit of Thunder

God saw all that He had made, and it was very good.
—Genesis 1:31 (NIV)

Mom and Dad didn't easily give up. After all, there was too much at stake. They loved one another in their own sort of way, I suppose. Deep down inside, they had a strong desire to honor their marital vows to love one another for better or worse, richer or poorer, in sickness and in health, until death do they part. Mostly though, they loved us kids and tried to stick it out through murky waters for our sakes. They genuinely believed they were doing what was best for their three young children in giving them the stability and security of a family unit that was all together under one roof. I can't fault them much for that. Whether or not it was the *right* or *wrong* decision, only God knows. It's really not that unusual in this game of life. I've heard about plenty of couples adopting similar reasoning. Maybe sometimes, it even works out for the best. At times, it may backfire. Almighty God can use either choice or outcome, I suppose.

Grandpa Daley always said that God will work all things out for good. He was not a fan of divorce. He said it wasn't God's plan. Although he loved us and was concerned for his daughter, son-in-law, and grandchildren, he encouraged the young couple to persevere for the most part until his concerns outweighed God's perfect plan for marriage and family. In the meantime, He guided his daughter to honor her marriage covenant and trust God for the restoration of all that was broken. So she did. Nowadays, they both beat themselves up a bit with all the *what-ifs*. After all, when tragedy strikes so close to home, it's easy for those who are left behind to spend the rest of their days on earth questioning every decision and life choice ever made. These things just can't be predicted, of course, and the simple truth is, sometimes no one is to blame. Unfortunately, accidents and tragedies just happen. Other times, it really doesn't matter if a decision or life choice was right or wrong. God's will is God's will. Although a perfect, holy, and loving Almighty Father surely doesn't *cause* tragedy, unfortunately, every once in a while, He does allow it. At times, we creatures on earth come to understand why He does what He does. Other times, we never quite figure it out this side of eternity. His ways are not our ways, and His thoughts are not our thoughts. Grandpa Daley always said that Almighty God works in mysterious ways and works *all* things together for the good of those who love Him and are called according to His purposes. So I guess one could reasonably conclude that *if* God does allow tragedy to strike close to home, He must have a very good reason and purpose. I might even go as far as to say that those going through the aftermath are indeed called according to His great purposes as the Almighty labors night and day without slumber, taking what was intended by a very real adversary to destroy and use it all for good.

Personally, if you ask me, and some of you weren't asking, I've grown to learn that the bigger the magnitude of storm that makes landfall in our backyards, the greater God's purpose is for the lives of those involved. At least, that's how it seems from the peephole in my front door. But then again, I'm surely not God. We can all be grateful for that. That God is God, and I am not. Some mess I'd have this world in if I were in control. I suppose that's why He limits the things He gives me control of. Far be it for me to be the judge. At one time, I thought I wanted that job. I eventually realized it wasn't all it was cracked up to be. It isn't easy when filled with sin and flaws, and flesh gets in the way of the supernatural realm to decide who of all of God's children matters to God and who does not. I shudder to think of being placed in a position where I may be forced to choose between my own children, even if they don't always do the right things. I still love them and would take their place if it came to me or them. There isn't anything they could do that would make me love them less, let alone think about life without them in it or worse yet, damn them to hell. When I stop to ponder, this really is amazing grace! Back to what I was saying, I digress from time to time. I think this amazing grace, the good news I've heard it called, is precisely the well-formed hypothesis we intend to form some sort of conclusion to on this journey together. If life's circumstances somehow lead us off track, how can we also, through those same circumstances that seemingly led us off course, end up on the predestined track, a highway to heaven of sorts? Well, we touched on that earlier. I guess that's where we're eventually heading, just as soon as we get there.

Back to Texas, the place we would depart from as Dad retired from the US Air Force. Our family moved back to the small hometown in Upstate New York where we were from and all our extended family still resided. Perhaps being back in the place where roots were deeply grounded, with the support system of parents, grandparents, aunts, uncles, and cousins, would be some sort of saving grace to the condition our family was in. It was Thanksgiving Day in 1977 when Mom, Dad, Greggie, Jimmy, and I boarded a U-Haul moving truck and left the little green house in White Settlement, Texas, trading military family life for a more traditional civilian lifestyle in the hometown we planned to settle down in and plant roots. We moved to a small rural community in the countryside, nearby both sets of extended family members. However, later that year as Old Man Winter returned to the northeast with a vengeance, the white two-story colonial in the woods could not stand up against the frigid, below-zero temperatures that bluster through Central New York. Perhaps the quaint white house that appeared to have beauty on the surface and outer shell lacked a solid foundation and the fortification of insulation within the deeper layers of the facade. Thus, it lacked the necessary safeguards from the wintry elements. There was a perplexing foundational life lesson in the structural erection of that cottage in the woods.

After our family endured a bitter winter, we moved out of the house and settled even deeper into the country in Dad's native town.

It was only a short fifteen-minute drive from Mom's hometown where most of her immediate family members lived. Dad loved animals of any kind and dreamed of owning a farm to house them one day. Mom had been raised on a farm. Her father was a dairy farmer. So continuing forward with life on a farm wasn't unfamiliar territory for her. Since the pair had dated throughout high school, Dad had his fair share of exposure to farm life as he was often at Mom's childhood farmhouse during his teen years. Ironically, our new home on the farm was another green ranch similar to one we left behind in Texas. Dad took a job at a local gun-making factory, and Mom spent her days raising three young children and tending to the affairs of our household and farm.

Brother, Jimmy, and I loved frolicking in the playroom in the back of our new home. Mom would often remind us to clean up our toys scattered over every square inch of the playroom. It was a room for toys, after all. Though obedient for the most part, we were normal kids. I don't know very many ordinary children who find enjoyment in the daunting task of cleaning up mounds of disheveled toys. So Mom did what any other busy, full-time mother of three children, all under the age of five years old, would do. She chose her battles carefully and sometimes simply shut the door. "Out of sight, out of mind" can be a very useful tool in an overwhelmed mother's tool belt. On warmer, sunny days, Mom often took my brothers and I down the road just a mile or so to the local elementary school and allowed us to play and get our energy out on the school playground. Jimmy was only a baby but he enjoyed it when Mom pushed him ever so tenderly on the swing that had a baby seat. Sometimes, Brother and I would beg our mother for a turn to push our baby brother. However, when we pushed him as high as we liked to swing, "'Til our feet touched the clouds," we used to say, Mom would remind us that he was only a baby and encouraged us to find another activity to do together. So we did.

Brother would sometimes stomp the dirt with one sneakered foot, and with his hand on his hip, he complained, "*Awww*, man!" After all, he was the baby up until Jimmy joined the family. Now he was stuck right exactly in the middle, not the oldest and with an older sister always bossing him around and no longer the baby. He struggled a bit to find his identity in his ever-changing family. Regardless, he loved both of his siblings very much and was always kind, gentle, and tender-hearted toward his new baby brother. As most children do when a new baby sibling turns their world upside down, he secretly wondered if Mommy and Daddy could just return him to the stork that sent him without a receipt or return mailing address. But he never said it aloud. He consistently showered our baby brother with love and affection in tangible ways. He enjoyed helping Mom as she fed baby Jimmy. Sometimes he needed to be reminded to be gentle as he shoved the nipple a little too far and forcefully into the back of Jimmy's throat. He often allowed Jimmy to clench his finger with his tiny little fist as Greggie smiled with gritted teeth and said aggressively, "Hi, baby brother!"

Nonetheless, Brother quickly let me boss him around as I prodded him, "Come on, Brother! Let's go on the spinning thing!"

Brother and I would make our way to the merry-go-round where we enjoyed taking turns twirling one another until we were both dizzy. We were like most siblings at that age. We were best friends and playmates, but we also had an occasional quarrel. As is the case with most children, the conflict would pass after a few minutes then we would be right back to playing together as if nothing happened. Kids don't seem to hold on to their grudges as we adults do. I suppose that's a gift in the grand scheme of life's troubles.

Speaking of kids and life's troubles, there was that one day when the three of us spent the night at Grandma and Grandpa Daley's house, as we often did. One beautiful, sunny, spring day, Grandma was making pancakes for breakfast as she often did. Two of their own eight children were still living at home and in grade school. The others were grown and married with their own children. On this particular day, the youngest, Dorothy (named after her mother, Grandma Daley) was instructed to go upstairs and wake her sister Melanie for school. Apparently, Melanie, a teenager at the time, didn't want to wake up and get ready for school. Although I don't suppose a teenager desiring to sleep in is all that uncommon. Dorothy did what any younger sister would do. She went to her mother and tattled on her older sister. "Mooom! Melanie ain't coming!"

Before Grandma Daley could respond or get to the bottom of the stairs to holler up at Melanie, Brother was standing in his crib at the top of the stairs. Only about two and one half years old and barely able to speak in complete sentences, he gave his two cents. "She ain't comin'? In dis wetta?" He was referring to the weather as the warm sun shone from the east windows. He was a smart and observant little fella at his young age, somehow a comedian, though not necessarily intending to be. He kept his large family laughing, sometimes under their breath since occasionally, it wasn't always necessarily appropriate behavior to be laughing at for an adult authority figure.

There was so much to love about living on a farm for young children. All three of us loved animals in general, but Brother was especially fond of animals. He was all boy. He loved playing in the mud and from time to time, even toddled through an occasional manure pile with the olive-green, rubber farm boots he usually wore. They resembled grandpa's. I suppose that was part of the reason he had an attachment to them. Somehow the boy in him just loved those olive-green boots that came almost all the way up to his little skinned knees. Maybe it was so that he could walk through the mud and manure piles on the farm with better reason. He certainly didn't mind. He just kept right on walking, manure and all. It could have been a bit intentional. He did have a slightly mischievous side. The only thing he was likely more attached to than the boots was his Hot Wheels trike. Oh, how he enjoyed peddling that little trike around the oval-shaped, gravel-and-dirt driveway at the front of the house. "Mom! Mom! Watch me!" He would excitedly shout as he spun his trike through the driveway, kicking up a cloud of dust that would linger above him. Mom faithfully watched. The sequence often bore repeating as moments later, he shouted yet again, "Mom! Mom! Watch this!" Mom attended to each and every stunt while also holding baby Jimmy.

Even though little Greggie had a bit of a mischievous side, he was also obedient. He knew his boundaries and that he wasn't allowed near the road with his trike. He never attempted to cross the boundary lines of the dusty trail he blazed in the oval driveway. Borders and boundaries are put in place by loving parents for their child's protection. If only Brother continued to stay within the boundary lines of safety and protection.

As much as he loved to be outside and play in the dirt, little Greg Jr. also had a gentle, compassionate side. He loved his family and animals almost just as much. He loved living on a farm where he could interact with animals often in the backyard, although there were mostly pigs on our farm. Dad sold them at auctions occasionally to make extra profit for our family. There were two pigs in particular, male and female, that we were drawn to. We named them Adam and Eve. Eve eventually had piglets, fourteen tiny ones. Sadly, one of the little piglets was born with deformities and didn't make it, but all the others did. Brother loved going to the barn and pigpen where the pigs were housed. He liked feeding them grain from his tiny little hands. He giggled as their wet noses tickled his palms.

At an auction one day, Dad bought a horse and brought it home on a cattle truck. Brother and I had begged for a horse for a while. Mom was less than thrilled about the newest addition to the family. She said that they had enough animals already. On the other hand, Brother and I were overjoyed about our new pet. The horse was mostly dark chocolate-brown with just a little bit of white. He was silky, shiny, and stoic. I named him Thunder. I thought it was a fitting name because he sounded like thunder when he ran. We couldn't wait to put a saddle on his back and ride him in the field of buttercups behind the barn. As much as Mom was not a fan of Dad bringing a horse home, she was equally not fond of the idea of allowing Brother and I to ride Thunder. Though soon enough, she allowed us to ride the stallion, of course, with Dad leading at our side. After all, there was really no reason for Mom's anxiety; that is, until that old Thunder gave her cause to worry. For no particular rhyme or reason, Thunder took off running through the field one day, which wouldn't have been a problem, except for the fact that I was harnessed on his back. I was only five years old, petite, and unable to hold on against the power and speed of the stallion. I fell off, landing on my back in the field. Mom and Dad ran to my rescue. Thankfully, there were no serious injuries. I made it through the accident unscathed, other than the emotional impact and fear. Thunder certainly didn't make it easy to earn the trust of our mother. However, she also knew that we loved the horse so she allowed him to stay, of course with some strict precautions and guidelines in place.

All in all, we had Adam, Eve, and all their offspring; Thunder; a whole lot of chickens and ducks; Dooley, a red Springer Spaniel; and a black cat named Jemima. For a little boy like Brother who absolutely loved animals, heaven on earth was right in his backyard. That following winter, we had winter storms, meteorologists refer to as Nor'easters, which essentially is just a fancy word for what they really are—blizzards. As the cold winds raged against the family farm, the snow measured in feet, rather than inches. Snowplows in the North Country plowed the roadways that built up mountainous snowbanks. The steep banks combined with snowdrifts created visibility deficits that made it nearly impossible for the driver of an oncoming snowplow to see the family dog, Dooley, as he chased the snow falling to the ground. News of Dooley's death by an oncoming snowplow was devastating for the entire family. It was especially shattering to my brothers and me since we had grown so attached to our furry companion, friend, and playmate. Our beloved Dooley was gone. Dad buried him in the field behind the house where he loved to run and roll in the grass on hot summer days.

Sadly, our family's troubles didn't stop there. Dad continued battling alcoholism until it finally got the best of him. Mom came home one day to find him nearly unconscious on the living room floor. She was beyond angry and at her wit's end as she assumed that he was passed out on the floor because of drinking too much, as the occasion would occur from time to time. This time though, something was just not right. Mom called Dad's sister Kim who lived right down the road. The sisters-in-law made a decision to call an ambulance. Dad was taken to the large Veteran's Medical Center about an hour-and-a-half-drive away since he was a veteran and also because hospitals in larger cities outside of their small rural town were a little better equipped to handle medical emergencies of serious magnitudes. This was indeed one of those instances.

The human body has a unique way of alerting us if we have had too much or too little of something. Dad's body was clearly sending a message loud and clear that the excessive alcohol was taking a toll on his organs. For lack of better medical terminology, his stomach organ had essentially "blown up," causing critical internal bleeding. He was taken into emergency surgery where literally, half of his stomach was removed while the other half was spared. His life was saved but he was not out of the woods yet. He sustained substantial internal bleeding, causing him to slip into a coma. He remained in the hospital for several weeks. Mom's oldest brother Bill (her father's namesake), his wife, and six children lived nearby the medical center. Mom, my brothers, and I stayed with Uncle Bill, Aunt Andrea, and their family on and off throughout the duration of Dad's hospital stay.

Uncertain of the future or if and to what extent her husband would recover and unable to manage the farm on her own with three small children, Mom made arrangements for the animals. Some were sold and given to relatives as she prepared to sell the farm and move to a house that was for sale near her parents that she had been interested in for a while. My brothers and I were saddened by the loss of our farm animals we loved so much. None of the animals were easy to say good-bye to. However, Adam and Eve (the pigs) and Thunder the horse were especially most difficult to part with. I don't know that we ever saw Adam and Eve again, but we occasionally saw a little bit of Thunder. The dark-brown stallion was going to be staying with Uncle Art, Grandpa Daley's brother-in-law as he owned enough acreage for the horse to trot around. Arrangements were made for us to occasionally visit and ride the pony. Although we were saddened from parting ways with the pigs and Thunder, we looked forward to the new journey in our new home, not so far out in the country and less than a mile down the road from our grandparents we loved so dearly. I guess that's what folks mean by the term *bittersweet*. This was one of such occasions. I had heard grown-ups all around me talk about how resilient children were. I secretly hoped they were right. Brother, Jimmy, and I had been through so much already.

6

The Plant

Plant the good seeds of righteousness, and you will harvest a crop of love.
—Hosea 10:12 (NLT)

Our new residence was located on Plant Road, however, locals commonly called the neighborhood the Plant. There was no other fanciful reasoning for the nickname, such as exotic plants in beautiful, blossoming botanical gardens or old oak trees of wisdom and knowledge. However, there was a beautiful weeping willow on the far corner of our front yard. We eventually planted an oversized vegetable garden in our backyard. Other than those factors, there really is no garden of Eden like the original. The Plant was a neighborhood filled with sounds of children playing altogether on warm summer days. Our first ever two-story, four-bedroom home was our favorite family home of all. This was to be the place where we would settle down and plant roots as a family.

Dad recovered from his life-threatening encounter with alcohol and returned to a new home. A new home was not the only significant change in his life. Dad also decided that his battle with alcoholism was over. He would no longer allow the bottle to take control of his life. He kept that commitment for many years. I often heard him in conversation with others, referring to himself as a recovering alcoholic. His wife and family were proud of his vow to abolish alcohol from their lives. His three children were most proud of our father's lifestyle change. In fact, we could often be heard boasting to strangers we met at school, the grocery store, or church that our dad used to be an alcoholic but that he quit drinking, and wasn't anymore.

I was going to begin first grade in my new school that fall. Brother would begin attending preschool. Jimmy was a toddler. Life was pretty good on the Plant. There was no shortage of children to play with in the neighborhood. It wasn't long before my brothers and I met all the neighborhood children. The family next door to ours, the Hagartys, had four children whom eventually became our best friends. There was nothing at the end of Plant Road but a dead-end sign. Well, that is, unless you counted the dirt road about midway between the entrance and the dead-end sign. With no asphalt and only gravel and dirt, that road would eventually lead a traveler to another part of town, deep into the country where the blackflies were so bad, you'd be eaten alive if you dared venture outside in that neck of the woods without being slathered in bug repellant. That part of the country would come to bear great significance, in more ways than one.

At this point, I reckon we spent our summer days much like other children our age did in the late seventies and early eighties. The beautiful, bellowing, weeping willow tree on the corner of our front yard became a treasured haven for me. I loved to lay a blanket under the draping branches and read a book or crochet, which I had recently learned how to do. When it wasn't being used as my secret garden, my brothers and I used the shade of the branches as a storefront for our lemonade business. We sold the refreshing yellow drink there for ten cents a plastic cup. Of course, those were different days when it was considered safe to raise a family during a time when neighbors still looked out for each other's children, and the philosophy that "it takes a village to raise a child" was still unspoken yet understood. Most people who stopped for an after-work refresher on their commute home wouldn't ask for change as they gave us a quarter, fifty cents, and sometimes a whole dollar on a good day. Very few passersby gave a dime, the actual amount listed on the sign, free of the added surcharges and taxes more common now. After all, those were simpler times. It was a generous small town in the country that some referred to as Timbuktu, where everyone really did know your name.

In fact, Grandma and Grandpa Daley were the local newspaper deliverers for the *Evening Times* in addition to dairy farming. They passed through on their way home each day. They were indeed their grandchildren's best, most faithful, and highest-paying customers. Sometimes they'd even stop to visit and bring us a big gallon-sized jar of fresh cow's milk from their livestock that day with a thick layer of cream on the top. From time to time, if we were especially lucky, my brothers and I took turns riding along on the paper route with our grandparents. We loved placing the rolled up local daily publication in each newspaper box at every customer's residence we pulled up next to on back country roads. Our favorite part about going on the paper route with Grandma and Grandpa Daley was stopping at the country store because we were allowed to pick out an ice cream treat from the store's freezer. We had a tight bond with Grandma and Grandpa Daley, but we also had a close relationship with Grandma and Grandpa Foster. More so Grandma Foster than Grandpa Foster. Grandpa Foster loved his children and grandchildren in his own way, I suppose. However, he was dealing with his own demons of alcoholism and the effects of that on himself as well as the family who loved him. He was in the logging business and worked long hours in the deep woods of North County. He spent his days cutting down trees then stacking and chaining the logs on large logging trailers, which were sold to local businesses for lumber and papermaking. Grandma Foster worked at a local shoemaking factory. During times when she wasn't working full time, she babysat us when Dad was at work and Mom had appointments on the calendar and eventually when she returned to work.

Grandma and Grandpa Foster lived nearby as well. Their home was a trailer that Grandpa Foster built a log cabin addition on with wooden front and side porches. We loved spending time with both sets of grandparents and did so often. One benefit we had in visiting Grandma and Grandpa Foster's house that we looked forward to was walking up the road to a local country store called Curly and Anita's. I don't know if Curly and Anita's store was officially the name on the deed to the property, but that's what it was known as to the locals who knew the store's owners, Curly and Anita. We often begged Grandma Foster on long summer days, "Grandma, can we go to Curly and Anita's store and buy some penny candy?"

She would usually say yes and give us some pocket change. She stood on the side porch and hung laundry on the clothesline as she watched us walk just a block up the street still within sight to the country store. On that side porch, Grandma could usually be found on hot summer days in the northeast. She was a sun bug and loved lounging on her outdoor recliner in her bikini and soaking up the rays. Some folks would have found humor in the fact that a woman who was Grandma to many grandchildren could likewise be found sporting a bikini on the side porch that was visible from the main highway in town. Her grandchildren didn't seem to find it unusual. That was just something that was commonplace in our world. Grandma Foster was tall and slender and always had bronzed skin, especially in the summer months. Conversely, Grandma Daley was short, overweight, and very modest. She could usually be found most days wearing long, floral dresses in every color of the rainbow. She had large arms with skin that sagged down from her triceps. Her arms were my favorite place to rest my head as I snuggled with her on the sofa where she enjoyed watching the six o'clock evening news with Bill Worden. I often told Grandma, "Your arms are the softest pillows, Grandma. They are just like pie dough." I kneaded and squeezed them with my fingers that barely had nails because of a pretty severe nail-biting habit. I can't imagine that statements, such as arms resembling that of pie dough, were much of a compliment to a woman's vanity, but Grandma didn't seem to mind—at least, not outwardly.

Back to Curly and Anita's country store. My brothers and I would walk up the steps to the front porch of that old store where we were known on a first-name basis and make a beeline to the penny candy bins. The store's owners would give us each a small paper sack, and we would begin placing Swedish Fish, gummy raspberries, and half dollars, as well as other various assorted candies in our brown bags. We then excitedly approached the checkout area to pay for our bags of candy. We liked to make our purchases separately. I suppose it would have been easier for convenience sake for the cashier to ring them all up at once, but the cashiers never complained—not to the children anyway. They smiled and patiently counted each piece of candy one bag at a time and one tiny little customer at a time. Although we stood on our tippy toes, our little heads barely peeked over the counter. We would then proceed out the screen door of the country store. Each patron smiled and waved as we passed by, and we smiled and waved back. We happily proceeded back down the sidewalk and on to Grandma Foster's house, sometimes with a little skip in our step as we reached in our bags and savored each piece of candy that cost us only one penny each. Sometimes we even traded a Swedish Fish for a gumball with one another. After all, what someone else has in their possession often looks better than the blessings in our very own hands. Occasionally, our happy skipping quickly became fearful running when we heard the loud rumbling of Harley Davidson motorcycles approaching from a motorcycle gang called Hell's Angels. The three of us would run for our lives when the motorcade passed through. I can't imagine the group intended to harm children in any way. Nonetheless, I can't help but wonder if an occasional man with a long gray beard and braided ponytail under their black helmets wearing matching black leather vests with patches and sporting tattoos on their biceps may have secretly gained some amount of gratification as they chuckled at these three wee ones running faster than their little feet could keep up.

Brother, the mischievous one, just loved to rile up Grandma Foster. Obedient and compassionate yet slightly mischievous, he always found it comical to ruffle our grandmother's feathers. Not that Jimmy and I didn't ever have a bad day or even find it funny when Brother ruffled Grandma's feathers. We were just a bit more discreet in our outward displays. Secretly, we laughed and giggled amongst ourselves, just enough to encourage further misbehavior, but we took great effort to ensure Grandma didn't notice. Somehow, Brother's mischief would mysteriously come out with a vengeance early in the morning after we were dropped off and he would become well-behaved and apologetic as the clock neared three o'clock when

Mom would get out of work for the day. Most days, it worked like a charm. Brother begged with puppy dog eyes, "Please, Grandma, don't tell on me. I promise I'll be good next time!" Somehow she usually fell into his trap with those sad eyes that naturally accented the cute little freckles on his face. Grandma seemingly developed a slight case of temporary amnesia for a few moments, just long enough to fail to remember to give our mother a bad report.

Indeed, having both sets of grandparents nearby and able to spend a lot of time with them was a blessing. The double blessing was that our great grandparents were still living. Well, not on my mom's side of the family. Unfortunately, Mom's grandparents had already gone home to be with the Lord. However, Dad's grandparents were still alive. Although elderly, they were very active in our lives. Grandma Foster's mother and stepfather, Grandma Hall and Gramp Ben, basically raised Dad as a child. As I briefly mentioned earlier, Grandpa Foster was an alcoholic and became quite violent and abusive when alcohol got the best of him. For some odd reason, Dad seemed to take a lot of the brunt of his father's rage. His grandmother, Grandma Hall, was intolerant of her son-in-law's abuse of her precious grandson. So in addition to their role as his grandparents, Grandma Hall and Gramp Ben became parental figures in Dad's life. Organically, since Dad was so close to his grandparents, so were my brothers and I. We spent a lot of time at Great-Grandma and Grandpa Hall's farm home in the country not far from where we lived. It was a beautiful brick home on scenic green pastures with a white barn off to the side of the house.

There was also Great-Grandma Grace. Oh, how we loved her. She was Dad's grandmother on his father's side (Grandpa Foster's mother). Her husband was George Foster Sr. He was an avid hunter and fisherman, so much so that he was even featured in an outdoor sports magazine for rabbit hunting back in his day. He was the grandson of the famous Nat Foster. We read about him in history class at our school. He was known as a great Indian fighter during the American Indian War and was widely responsible for settling most of the land of the Foster's ancestors in Upstate New York. He died when Dad was about fourteen years old so we never had the privilege of meeting him. Sometimes from the stories Dad and his family told as well as what we learned in history class, it felt as though we did. Grandma Grace more than made up for his absence. She was loving but very stern. Some may have even thought of her as a bit feisty. She owned a very popular diner from 1952–1977 in the town we called home. In fact, it was right next door to her home, bearing the family last name called Foster's Drive Inn. It was a happy place to be, and the food was so spectacular, people drove from all over North Country and beyond to eat at the establishment. It was well-known for burgers, hot dogs, and fried chicken, but it was famous for Grandma Grace's Mexican hot sauce and spaghetti sauce. In fact, her Mexican hot sauce and spaghetti sauce were so delicious and famous that they were sold at local supermarkets, such as Contino's, for many years. To this day, only Uncle Bruce, one of the twins she birthed (Bruce and Brian), has the recipe to her Mexican hot sauce. He was sworn to secrecy as she handed him the handwritten recipe card. She gave the order, "Not one word." She was also well-known for her homemade pies. She awoke at 4:30 am every morning to begin baking. The drive-in atmosphere welcomed motorcyclists from all over the area and beyond. There was a dine-in option, of course, where the jukebox played all the hits. A quarter played three songs. It was equally enjoyable to dine outside or even in the car. It was a drive-in so patrons could pull in and order at the window and dine in their vehicles. It was understandable that my brothers and I enjoyed visiting Grandma Grace. Bearing a striking resemblance in the eyes, our bond was undeniable. We loved playing at her house and restaurant even more so than we loved eating her famous cooking.

On summer days when we were not at Grandma Foster's house eating penny candy, outrunning the Hell's Angels, or delivering newspapers in the Chevrolet Caprice Classic alongside Grandma and Grandpa Daley, my brothers and I could be found around the Plant. We had three mock bases set up in our side yard for baseball games with all the neighborhood children. There was an above-ground swimming pool in our backyard where we played Marco Polo with our cousins and neighborhood friends on hot sunny days. In the far backyard behind the chain-link fence, we labored many hours building a fort with spare lumber and materials we gathered up from the surrounding woods. Once the clubhouse—constructed of random planks and nails—was complete, we hung out in it often. In fact, my brothers spent such a considerable amount of time in our fort that Dad asked them what exactly they did during all the hours they spent bunkered in their humble abode in the woods. They were a bit overly honest in their reply as kids often are. "Oh, we say curse words and spit, Dad." Barely able to keep a straight face at their honest reply, Dad further interrogated about why they retreated to the fort to say curse words and spit. They rationalized that it was against the household rules to do those things, but in "their own dwelling," which they built from scratch with their hands, it wasn't against the rules. Thus the two obedient but a bit mischievous boys could break the rules without necessarily breaking the rules, if you know what I mean.

Speaking of mischief and breaking the rules, there was that instance where little Greggie stretched the boundary lines a bit farther than he should have. Mom found a few bloodstains in his GI Joe underwear one day while doing laundry. She asked brother, who was seven or eight years old at the time, about the stains, but he couldn't offer much explanation. Mom took him to good old Dr. Burke, the local family practitioner who had delivered almost every baby in the county. He wasn't very fancy, didn't always have the greatest bedside manner, and practiced medicine based on simple, old-fashioned remedies without the modern technology and practices of this day and age. To his credit, those weren't very modern times and technology wasn't what it is today. He did seem to have a solution to just about any medical concern and problem presented to him. He was talented in his craft. Much of the time, he based his fees on the type of car any given patient drove to his office. I guess he figured if you could afford a luxury vehicle, you could certainly afford to pay full price. However, in our family's case, we certainly didn't drive anything fancy. We owned a brown 1972 Chevy Chevelle that had the passenger door riveted shut as a result of little Greggie falling out on one occasion. The door latch was rusted and opened one day as we rounded a sharp corner and Brother fell out. I suppose Dad riveting the door shut was a bit of an overreaction, but it did solve the problem even if another was created by no longer being able to enter and exit the vehicle from the passenger side. The condition of that old Chevelle sure did make for an economical office visit to Dr. Burke. He only charged our family about five dollars for an appointment. On this occasion, Dr. Burke handed Mom a sterile plastic specimen container and instructed her to collect a urine sample from her son.

Upon returning home, Mom handed the container to Brother and told him what to do the next time he needed to go to the bathroom. He followed Mother's instructions and soon after returned the specimen cup to her. When Brother handed what appeared to be a blood-tinged urine specimen to Mom, she panicked and took him to the emergency department at the local hospital. The ER physician ordered some lab work, beginning with the urine specimen that had been brought in. After a while, the nurse returned to the exam room and asked mom if the specimen she brought in had been tampered with in any way. Mom was confused as to why she would be asked such an absurd question and responded that it had not been. The physical examination and lab test results were normal. Medical personnel determined that the specimen had been tampered with in some way and that little Greg Jr. was fine, medically speaking. At home, Mom interrogated, "Okay, where is it?" Brother ran upstairs to his bedroom with Mom following closely behind. He went to the bookshelf on his twin bed and reached for his Easter basket where he had some leftover candy stashed away. From the basket, he took out a tiny plastic bottle of red food coloring and handed over the piece of evidence. Mom confiscated the red dye. "Why did you do that?" Mom asked.

"I just wanted to see what the inside of the hospital looked like, and I wanted to ride on the elevator" Brother explained.

"Well, why didn't you just tell me? I would have taken you there to see what it looked like!"

Mom and Dad were relieved that a life-threatening medical diagnosis had been avoided. Life on the Plant continued. On any given day when we weren't playing in our fort or selling lemonade, we did what most other kids back in the early eighties did. We lounged around on Saturday mornings, eating bowls of sugary cereal and watching our favorite Saturday morning cartoons. The Smurfs, Care Bears, Strawberry Shortcake, Rainbow Brite, Power Rangers, and GI Joe were our favorites.

Dad eventually left his job after many years at the gun factory and opened his own mechanic and body shop in our two-stall garage. Sometimes my brothers and I watched him as he worked on cars. Mom loved to cook and bake. Sometimes we abandon the garage and joined our mother in the kitchen. We stood on kitchen chairs pushed up to the countertops and assisted her. Brother, Jimmy, and I took turns adding the ingredients, eggshells and all, or mixing and stirring things. Sometimes she'd let us lick the beaters from the mixer. There were only two beaters and three children. So the odd child out would get to lick the mixing spoon instead, which didn't necessarily mean being shortchanged. Mom usually put a little extra batter on the spoon to make up the difference. She didn't worry all too much about things like raw egg consumption and salmonella. Those were simpler times before eating organic and gluten-free became a trend. She chose her battles wisely, and giving her children an occasional special treat was more important to her than the rare occasion a case of salmonella made the news.

Family life wasn't perfect on the Plant. I don't reckon I have ever met a perfect family yet, but it was some of our better times. Eventually, all three of us kids were school age and looked after one another in passing in the hallways of our school, in the cafeteria, and during recess. There was something recognizably unique about our sibling bond. Many long for it; few have it; and unfortunately for others, some lose it, realizing just how significant the relationship was when the void cuts so deep. I don't have much of an explanation for the extra-special bond we shared. Maybe it was because we had been through so much in our years of innocence that we looked to one another for peace and comfort during the tumultuous times. As the oldest, the big sister, I was naturally motherly. I guess God just somehow fashioned me that way in my mother's womb. I possessed an instinct that mothered, nurtured, and protected my little brothers. Since I naturally did so, whether my younger brothers wanted me to or not (I could be a little extra bossy at times), they gravitated toward it. Maybe the more accurate analogy would be that they tolerated it. Either way, tit for tat, it doesn't really matter the how or why. It just was, and it was good. I would almost venture to say, it was somehow God's providence and grace in our lives. He was already very much at work. After all, there was a plan to use each of us mightily one day to accomplish His own special purposes. We didn't know it then. We do now, I suppose.

7

Frontside Handplant

"Plant your roots in Christ and let him be the foundation of your life. Be strong in your faith, just as you were taught. And be grateful."
—Colossians 2:7-9 (CEV)

While her children were in school during the day, Mom spent her days cleaning, doing laundry, cooking, and baking. Every day when yellow school bus number 36 pulled up in front of our home after school, my brothers and I raced to the back door in the kitchen where Mom baked us a special treat. We looked forward to it, and it sort of became tradition. Mom wasn't concerned much about us having too much sugar as some moms do these days. These home-baked goodies were made from scratch with love. She's grateful nowadays that she didn't sweat the small stuff like giving her kids too much sugar, especially knowing now what she didn't know then. Sometimes it's those cherished memories that are all we have left to hold on to.

When Mom wasn't busy homemaking, she spent time with her middle sister, Sundi, also a stay-at-home mom. They went shopping, nothing fancy, just the local shops and occasionally out to lunch. During the summer months when we didn't have school, Aunt Sundi's two children, Sundi Rose and Courtney, along with my brothers and I, joined Mom and her sister. Sometimes we played at one another's homes and forts; other times we enjoyed swimming and playing on the shores at Pine Lake. At the same lake, there was also a campsite.

Uncle Buster and Aunt Sundi owned a camper that attached to their truck. All the cousins loved to pile in it for a weekend or even just a one-night camping extravaganza.

Sundi Rose and Courtney were two of over twenty first cousins on Mom's side of the family. On Dad's side, there were over a dozen first cousins. Mom was one of eight siblings; Dad was one of six. We came from a very large and very close lineage. Gatherings on both sides of the family were common and something we all very much looked forward to. In fact, our thirty-plus first cousins were very much our best friends. Holiday get-togethers were large, loud, hectic, and amazing all at the same time. It was tradition to go to Grandma and Grandpa Daley's house on big holidays such as Thanksgiving, Christmas, and Easter, where it was normal to find upwards of forty immediate family members seated around multiple tables. The cousins all looked forward to hide and seek, kickball, dodgeball, badminton, sledding, and snowman building. After spending time at Grandma and Grandpa Daley's house, we made our way to Grandma and Grandpa Foster's house. There an additional large family gathering of twenty to twenty-five immediate family members congregated for a meal and more of the same, while the cousins frolicked for the remainder of the day.

Halloween was an equally festive time of year in our community and school. Halloween costume parades, school Halloween parties, and, of course, trick-or-treating were events we looked forward to in fall, the season we loved in the northeast. There truly is nothing as beautiful as autumn in New York. It's very much everything the movies portray. Fall was beautiful in the mountainous part of the North Country, and the scenery was of rolling hills of green grass with views of red, orange, yellow, and purple foliage on large oak trees as far as the eyes could see. The sun shone bright and warm in the afternoons, yet the evenings and mornings were cool and crisp. Mom crafted one of a kind, home-made costumes for us. She wasn't the seamstress her younger sister Sundi was. However, she was creative in utilizing large cardboard boxes, glue, and colored paper to assemble makeshift Rubik's cubes and pine-green Christmas trees complete with strings of multicolored twinkling lights. We didn't have a lot of money to spare in the budget for a store-bought costume that would only be worn one night a year. So Mom used what was readily on hand in the closets and attic to dress me as an angel or princess, Greggie as an old lady or a cat, and Jimmy as a bunny or action figure. Our handcrafted costumes often won prizes in contests for originality and creativity.

Most Halloweens, trick-or-treating happened in bitter cold temperatures, and sometimes there was even a snow flurry or two. Mom,

Dad and us kids piled into our 1972 brown Chevy Chevelle and drove from home to home within our neighborhood and surrounding areas. Dad pulled up to the homes of the people we knew while Mom helped my brothers and me as we jumped out of the car and ran to each respective door in eager anticipation of the candy awaiting our bags on the other side. We were only allowed to go to the houses with the porch light on, which meant that the home was trick-or-treater-friendly. Sometimes the homeowner would sit on the front porch, greeting each costumed child. My brothers and I took turns knocking on the door as we enthusiastically exclaimed, "Trick or treat!" Someone on the other side of the door welcomed us, filling our bags with treats. Then we ran back to our car to be chauffeured to the next house.

Our favorite places to go to were our grandparents' homes where we received extra special treats. Grandma Daley sometimes pretended not to recognize us at first when we arrived on the front stoop dressed in our costumes. We liked to make her guess who we were, and she played along momentarily. After a few guesses, she correctly identified each of us beneath our disguises. Then we were instructed to open and hold out our sacks so that they could be filled to the brim with special candy treat bags, homemade popcorn balls, candy corn, and sometimes money—not much, mainly loose pocket change, but to three small children, it was as if we had struck gold.

Of course, there were also family cookouts, reunions, and various other gatherings outside of the major holidays. Uncle Buster and Aunt Sundi owned a summer home on a lake. Every summer, they hosted multiple events at the lake home: cookouts, swimming, fishing, fireworks, and gatherings on the water aboard the party barge.

Speaking of fishing, that was something mainly Greg Jr. and Jimmy enjoyed doing with our father. Perhaps, I felt a bit jealous about the amount of time my brothers enjoyed alone with Dad out on the shores of their favorite fishing spots. So one day, I asked Dad if he could take me fishing, just the two of us. Dad agreed to my terms of no brothers allowed and took me out. I caught a notable-sized bass that day. However, I was a girly girl at heart and not fond of touching the worm to put it on my own hook or taking the fish off the hook to throw it back in the lake. I was satisfied though. I had the special father-daughter time with my dad, doing something he typically did with his sons while I stayed home helping Mom.

This wasn't the only occasion I attempted to insert myself into something my brothers did with Dad. As the only girl in the family, I suppose I often felt like the odd man out, figuratively speaking. Greg and Jimmy joined a local Little League baseball team, and Dad was asked to coach. He agreed, and, of course, the boys were placed on his team. I wanted to be part of the team with my brothers and father so I asked if I could sign up too. Mom and Dad agreed, although my brothers weren't fond of the idea. After all, they played baseball in the backyard with me enough to know that I wasn't necessarily an asset to their team. Nonetheless, our parents signed me up, and I was placed on the same team with my dad as the coach and brothers as teammates. Our team's name was the Dodgers, and our uniforms were red and white. My brothers were talented baseball players. One played the position of pitcher and first baseman, and the other was pretty good behind the catcher gear. On the other hand, I could usually be found in the outfield, a long way out in the outfield. I wasn't very good at catching the balls that were batted in my direction. When it was my turn to bat, it wasn't any better. I usually didn't hit the ball and struck out after swinging and batting. I wasn't the athlete in the family, unlike my brothers who seemed to be born athletes. They would eventually become town football hall of fame inductees. But that was later down the road. For now, we're talking baseball. I moved on from the baseball field after that season, and both of my brothers were happy about that.

The one thing we looked forward to most was the trip from baseball practice or games in town back home to the Plant. The route from town to our neck of the woods was one that passed by a local burger and ice cream drive-in that was only open from April to September each year. It was a popular establishment in the summer months so it was common to run into an acquaintance in our small hometown when stopping by there. We weren't a wealthy family, but we weren't poor as church mice, as the old saying goes. We certainly fell below the line that falls somewhere right in the middle. Going out to eat or even out for ice cream was a treat and a pretty big deal. My brothers and I understood there were times of plenty and times of want. Dad worked on cars for a living. On months when there were more cars to work on, there were more opportunities for indulgences such as stopping by Green Acres for an ice cream cone. All three of us kids seemed to share a common favorite, a small chocolate and vanilla twist soft serve ice cream cone with rainbow sprinkles. Sometimes Brother ordered chocolate because Dad preferred chocolate and he always liked to duplicate him.

We were kids so we did what many kids do, I suppose. Brother and I set up the baby of the family to do our dirty work. We nudged him from either side as Jimmy sat in the middle of the back seat and whispered in his ear, "Ask Mom and Dad if we can stop at Green Acres for ice cream." Little Jimmy did as he was told by his two older siblings, unaware that he was being used as a pawn. "Dad?" Sometimes he'd ask Mom first. "Brother and Sissy wanna know if we can go to Green Acres!" Embarrassed that our baby brother gave us away, we stuttered (Greg sort of did so naturally) and denied any culpability, followed by an occasional punch on Jimmy's thigh or a dirty look. That would only give him further scandalous material to tattle about as he fussed and whined, "Brother and Sissy just hit me!"

Thus officially enlisting the involuntary employment of our parents as professional referees and judges as we three siblings battled it out like WWE in the back seat.

"He's looking at me!"

"Mom, she's looking at me!"

"Dad, Brother just hit me!"

"They just called me a little jerk!"

"He's sticking his tongue out at me!"

Mom and Dad let us duke it out amongst ourselves for the most part, usually ignoring our tattling on one another and requests for capital punishment for the one on trial. That is, until one of us spewed out statements that were intolerable. You know, *those* statements kids say in anger that they don't mean because they have yet to learn how to appropriately communicate their feelings and sort them out. "I hate you! I hope you die!" At which point of course, our parents, intercepted out of patience, and rightly so, "Hey! That's enough!" Usually, that was all it took to produce more appropriate behavior from us. We were seldom given spankings. It had to be a pretty serious infraction to enlist physical disciplinary action. A firm tone of voice was usually sufficient.

There was, of course, that one incident when the three of us piled into the front and back seats of our 1972 Chevrolet Chevelle, accidentally shifted into gear and haphazardly rolled backwards into the middle of route 29. Dad chased after us, flung open the driver's side door, and stopped the car just in the nick of time as oncoming traffic approached. We were most definitely lined up side by side to receive chastisement that day. Rightly so. After all, we placed our very lives in danger. Nonetheless, he hated spanking his children. I don't suppose any good parent enjoys disciplining their children regardless of how necessary it may be at the time. Of course, we weren't fond of the idea either. However, what we most hated and regretted were the statements we said to one another in fits of rage and anger. We later apologized and moved on as though nothing happened, but deep within our souls, we wished we had had better control of our tongues in the heat of the moment, especially years down the road. Those are the demons that have a way of staying with us.

It was a family tradition, just as much as our regular Sunday family dinners, to watch WWF WrestleMania. The boys especially looked forward to the airing of one of their favorite shows. In fact, Dad bought them tickets once to see a live show that was on tour in a nearby city. After hours of watching Andre the Giant, Hulk Hogan,

Jimmy "Superfly" Snuka, Ric Flair, and Jake "the Snake" Roberts pin each other down for three counts, we mimicked the wrestling superstars. My brothers and I ganged up on and tackled Dad to the ground, and a WrestleMania of sorts commenced live on our living room floor. All three of us piled on top of Dad until he eventually let us pin him down. It was also part of our tradition that Dad and my two brothers held me down and tickled me until I wet my pants. I had a history of laughing until that physical reaction occurred, which they took full advantage of. I usually got mad and stormed off to my bedroom. Mom wasn't fond of the pastime. She shouted, "Someone's gonna get hurt!" She was usually angry with Dad, more so than us. She reasoned that he was teaching us to fight. So we'd settle down a bit, but it sure was fun while it lasted.

There was also a drive-in movie theater just a half an hour out of town or so. Our family enjoyed making plans with other families within the neighborhood or within our extended family members to go as a group to the drive-in, caravan-style. Admission was five dollars per car back in the 1980s. Each car found a place to park next to a speaker to listen to the movie playing on the big screen in front of us on the far end of the field. All of the kids usually brought blankets and laid out on the field together in front of their respective cars and bickered over who was going to sit next to who to watch movies, such as *The Muppets Take Manhattan*. There was a concession stand where movie essentials such as popcorn, candy, and soda could be purchased. Usually, all the kids would put their movie treats together and evenly divide them between the group. It was a simple life, but it was a good life for the most part.

Remember that dirt and gravel road halfway up the Plant? As my brothers and I grew older, we spent a significant amount of time on that dirt road. Dad bought a motorcycle. Mom was equally as fond of that purchase as she was the time he brought home that old horse. During summer months, we loved taking turns on the motorcycle where we sat in front of Dad between the seat and the gas tank that was painted a beautiful turquoise blue with gold sparkles mixed in the paint that shimmered in the sunlight. Dad took us one by one from our driveway to the dirt road and back to the driveway.

It reminded me of the day our family was on our way to a nearby town to do some shopping. We took a back road from our home to another town about a half an hour away where larger retailers like Kmart and fast-food drive-throughs were located. Our hometown mostly consisted of little mom-and-pop stores. There was nothing on the back road but farm country. We were only about ten minutes from our destination when our vehicle seemingly ran out of gas. Broken down and out of gas on the side of an old country back road that lacked much through traffic, Dad instructed us to stay in the car while he walked to a nearby farmhouse to ask for assistance. After a while, we recognized Dad off in the distance coming toward us through a cornfield riding along with the farmer who owned the property. We giggled and laughed as we watched Dad standing on the back of that tractor with his hair blowing in the wind. The farmer gave us some extra gas he found in the barn, which we syphoned into the tank of our vehicle. It provided enough fuel to drive us to a nearby gas station.

Come to think of it, that same back country road we often traveled holds more than its fair share of memories. I think I may have mentioned back on the farm that Dad loved animals. My brothers and I equally loved them just as much or almost as much, especially Brother. So much so that I can think of several incidences when our family was traveling and discovered an injured animal along the roadside that had been hit by a passing vehicle. We always stopped to nurse the animal back to life. In the event that it was too late, we appropriately buried the animal nearby and held a roadside funeral service. We weren't always able to do such things, especially during winter months. One thing was for certain about winter in Upstate New York, to survive the long, cold, and snowy winters that plagued the North Country, it was essential to have the right toys. Dad found a good deal on a snowmobile. We got a little carried away one late winter afternoon as all three piled on the seat of the motorized snow sled. We were going a little faster than we should have been as we raced down Plant Road. As we approached the snow-covered dirt road, a mountainous snowbank was just ahead. Brother was driving and holding his frozen, glove-covered thumb on the throttle when he lost control of the sled. We hit the snowbank head on, bending the skis on the sled nearly vertical. Thankfully none of us were injured and somehow, we pushed and pulled until we dislodged the skis from the icy snowbank. Then we drove the damaged snowmobile back home where we had to report what happened.

Now that we're on the topic of winters on the snow-covered dirt road, there was also a pond back behind the trail called Mill Pond. In the winter, it froze over so we made it our own manmade ice skating rink. Mom wasn't any fonder of our newfound skating pond than she was any of the other things she found to be risky and dangerous. She feared that the ice would crack and we would fall in. If she only knew that as my brothers grew a little older and hence, a little more adventurous, they learned how to build a fire from sticks in the woods while attending Boy Scouts and Royal Rangers and occasionally did so back near the icy pond to keep warm as they ice fished. I don't know that Mom even knows that bit of information to this day. Depending on whether or not she reads every detail in this book will determine what she finds out. I'm not sure how much of this story Mom will be able to bear. There are some things that are just too painful for a mother to revisit. The boys learned how to build a fire in Royal Rangers, which may seem a bit of a mystery to those following along as to what in the name of Land of Goshen, as Grandma Daley would say, that might be.

Well, just as Almighty God's providence would have it, there was a little country church right directly across the street from our white, two-story home on Plant Road. My brothers and I were invited to vacation Bible school at the Assembly of God church one summer. We attended and enjoyed it. We learned Bible stories and songs, played games, made crafts, had snacks, and made new friends. Mom was very happy about that. She had been raised in a religious family and knew that having Christian friendships and influences for her children was certainly a good thing. Dad on the other hand, was not raised in a particularly religious family, although I do recall attending a local Methodist church on several occasions with Grandma Foster. Nonetheless, Dad didn't oppose our participation in church activities. He knew it certainly couldn't hurt our foundation or future.

After having an enjoyable experience there and meeting new friends, we continued going back on Sunday mornings for Sunday school. The reverend of the church, Pastor Jack Martin, had a special place in his heart for our family. Our family was equally fond of him and his family as well. He would come to bear greater significance in our lives than any of us were aware of at the time.

So we got involved in the Royal Rangers and Missionettes, a Boy Scout-Girl Scout-type Christian club for boys and girls that met each week at the church. We began earning our Royal Ranger and Missionette badges and getting more and more involved. As elders in the church became aware that all three of us had some amount of musical ability, we were invited to sing in the children's choir. Soon enough, we started performing solos, duets, and trios together on Sunday mornings during worship as well as in special events and holiday services. Most memorable were the occasions when I sang a song Grandma Daley asked me to sing as a solo special performance. It was called "I'm a Little Person in Jesus, He's a Big Person in Me," and my brothers performed a duet titled, "I'm in the Lord's Army." They were the cutest little auburn-haired, freckle-faced boys as they sang with choreographed hand motions, "I'm in the Lord's army. Yes, sir!" They saluted the congregation from the stage each time the chorus came around repeating their favorite verse of the song that they shouted loud and bold, "Yes, sir!" Our parents attended from time to time, especially on occasions when we performed.

I suppose Almighty God was likely busy at work behind the scenes and within our hearts during that season of life. To some extent, I would say He had His way. But then again, when does God not get His own way? It was very much a work in progress, incomplete yet in the works. He finishes what He starts. Grandpa Daley always told us that "He who began the good work in you is faithful and will complete it." I reckon Grandpa Daley was right. Although, even as wise and close with God as Grandpa Daley was, I don't think even he was prepared for how God would come to complete the good work He had begun. It certainly isn't how any of the family would have chosen to have God work in and through our lives.

While on the Plant, there were some notable outward evidences of inward workings of something greater, something supernatural. All three of us kids reported giving our hearts to Jesus at some point during our time at that little white church in the country or church-related events. Even Dad at some point later down the road had an encounter with his heavenly Father in that place. Perhaps the Plant was a place where good seeds of righteousness had been planted and began the germination process so that later on down the road, a different road, on a different track, a crop of love would be the harvest.

8

North Star

When they saw the star, they were overjoyed.
—Matthew 2:10 (NIV)

Well, all things have a beginning and an ending, I suppose. In much the same way, after about a decade on the Plant, it was time for our family to move on a little farther north. Mom wasn't particularly fond of moving. After all, for the most part, she loved the home where she raised her children for over ten years. It wasn't a perfect home—although some updating had been done—but it was a home filled with wonderful memories as well as not so wonderful memories.

In much the same way that it wasn't a perfect home, it wasn't a perfect marriage. There were ongoing marital problems. There were good days and bad days. Sometimes the bad days overshadowed the good days—or at least that's how it seemed. Then again, human nature has a peculiar way of paying more attention to and hyperfocusing more on all that is wrong in our lives than all that is right. Whether or not one sees the glass as half empty or half full is a matter of perspective and vantage point. Nonetheless, after several instances of separating and getting back together, Dad wanted a fresh start. Mom was not in favor of the decision, but she agreed that maybe something new was just what they needed.

Dad's brother-in-law, had family who owned a piece of property a couple of miles from the Plant. In fact, that old dirt and gravel road I mentioned in the previous chapter was a shortcut to the property. Mom and Dad purchased the two-acre plot of land, which included a foundation and basement that had already been constructed by previous owners. We sold our home on the Plant and packed up a decade's worth of memories, good and bad, and moved a little further north. The particular basement on two acres of green pastures was specifically located on North Road, which would become the address for our new start. Unfortunately, the reality is that sometimes the best intentions for new beginnings can fall short amidst the shattered glass of broken dreams and failed expectations. This specific fresh start was essentially the beginning of the end in more ways than one. The star that led us north would become both the *alpha* and the *omega*.

We utilized the basement on the land to serve as our temporary living quarters while Dad labored building the frame of the home. Sometimes Mom helped him. Occasionally, Mr. Hagarty, our old neighbor and friend from the Plant assisted Dad. Dad was a builder by trade at that stage of life. He worked for a large-scale roofing contractor and eventually started his own construction company. He was a capable homebuilder, however, with a full-time job and family coupled with a shoestring budget necessitating self-performing much of the building process independent of paid subcontractors, he was limited in the area of time and resources. Little by little, one two-by-four and nail at a time, within a few months, the one-story ranch home was framed, closed in, and the process of relocating from the temporary housing space of the basement to the permanent home mounted atop the foundation began. Greg, Jimmy, and I picked out our bedrooms and excitedly went to work decorating the newly constructed walls with posters of our favorite eighties and nineties Hollywood stars and rock stars. The great thing about fresh sheetrock walls that had yet to be spackled, sanded, primed, and painted was that we could even add a little extra pizazz of our own through artwork and graffiti.

Brother was a gifted artist. He loved to draw and shade and did so often. He had even gained the attention and favor of his school art teacher, Ms. Shapiro. She recognized artistic talent and ability in him that was unique. Likability was mutual. Greg enjoyed art class, and Ms. Shapiro was one of his favorite teachers. He sometimes was in trouble in school, not for anything serious in early high school years, but merely for being a class clown. However, Ms. Shapiro understood him. An artist herself, she just seemed to get it when it came to utilizing something one was passionate about to take the focus off other troubles in the world. Submerging oneself in a world that could be created according to preferences and ideal scenarios existing only in the creative imagination was therapeutic. Greg had good reason to do so. Our home life was falling apart before our eyes as our parents' marriage crumbled, and things were often tumultuous. I was a teenager, fifteen years old or so, and had begun dating. I focused on my relationship with a newfound high school sweetheart, which gave me solace. Jimmy was still young, only about eleven years old. Still a child, he stayed busy hanging out with friends, riding his bike into town, swimming and fishing at a nearby creek with a covered bridge, and just doing what boys do.

To avoid the exposure to our parents fighting at home, the three of us stayed with friends a lot. We also had a few favorite aunts and uncles we could turn to. I hung out with Aunt Dorothy a lot who was the youngest of Mom's seven siblings and only about five years older than me so it was a relationship that resembled more that of sisters than aunt and niece. There was also Aunt Kim who we called Aunt Me-Me, for short. She was Dad's youngest and only sister. All three of us sort of thought of Aunt Me-Me's home as our home away from home and were there often. Her house was just the place everyone seemed to feel comfortable gathering. It wasn't necessary to knock on the door before entering, and we knew there was never a shortage of a large supply of freeze pops in her freezer. We had permission to help ourselves to the assorted ice pops any time we wanted to. She always had a large pitcher or two of freshly brewed iced tea in the refrigerator that was strong enough to grow hair on your chest. Yet there was nothing more refreshing on hot summer days in Upstate

New York than a tall glass filled with ice and Aunt Me-Me's freshly brewed iced tea.

By this point, Grandma and Grandpa Foster had given up on the idea of staying married any longer. I can't say as I blame Grandma Foster. Her husband was not an easy man to be married to as were the demons he battled with. She moved in with her daughter, Aunt Me-Me so they were both available to us. Aunt Kim was married to Uncle Randy, and they had two daughters, Amanda and Kayla. We were equally as close to our first cousins—Mandy and Kay, we called them—by virtue of being at their home so often. After all, cousins make the best friends, second to siblings. I always like to say that siblings are God's way of giving us built-in best friends. Of course, first cousins are the next best thing. I acted in the role of big sister to my cousins, Mandy and Kay. I practically lived with them growing up. I loved being at Aunt Kim's home from the time she wed and moved into her own apartment. I enjoyed being there even more so once she had children. I loved babies and found joy in mothering Aunt Kim's babies.

While Jimmy was closer in age to Mandy and Kay and more of a peer, Greg took on the role of big brother and protector. He watched out for the girls in school. If anyone teased them for any reason, the wrath of Greg followed closely behind. That's just who he was. He was loyal to his family and naturally a born protector to those he loved and called family. Not only did the girls have Cousin Greggie to serve and protect them, but they also had an entire entourage of his closest buddies not far in the distance. In fact, his closest friends could commonly be found hanging out at Aunt Kim's house with Greggie as well. Known as the Kool-Aid house, it was the house that not only my brothers and I retreated to, but that of our friends as well, especially the group of boys Greg hung out with. Gerald, Richie, Sean, and Jim (not our brother Jimmy) were some of Greg's closest friends. On any given day, it was unlikely to see one without the others. As often as Greg hung out at Aunt Kim's home, the group of three or four friends were often with him. They played Nintendo with Grandma Foster. She loved to play Super Mario Brothers, and the boys enjoyed playing right alongside her. She was a skilled gamer, although she often relied upon the boys to get her to the next level. When they weren't playing Nintendo, they played cards at the kitchen table and sometimes watched movies. After all, unlike our home in the country where cable TV was not yet accessible, Aunt Me-Me's house was in town and had cable. I'm sure the fact that Aunt Kim never seemed to have a shortage of food and treats made her home popular amongst teens. She never really knew how many there would be for dinner on any given night. She didn't mind. It's just what it was, and it gave her great joy to have her nieces, nephews, and all their closest friends there. At Christmastime, Uncle Randy was known for his Chevy Chase, National Lampoon's Christmas-style festive lights and decor that outlined every square inch of their light-blue, two-story colonial home on Elm Street. Greg looked forward to working alongside Uncle Randy each year as they strung thousands of twinkling multicolored lights.

While Greg assisted in making all things merry and very, very bright, circumstances back on the home front continued deteriorating. It's not my business to talk about how or why my parents' marriage was falling apart at the seams. We all have skeletons in our closets. I suppose, some skeletons are bigger than others. For some, it isn't the size of the skeletons that take a toll on a marriage and family, but the parties in the marriage are just too exhausted to keep fighting dry bones any longer. Everyone has a limit, a boundary line that just can't afford to be crossed any longer. Mom and Dad's boundaries had been crossed and stretched so much, the lines had become blurry. Feelings faded and merely a mess remained. However, that is their story to tell. My role in recounting this narrative is to bring you through a sequence of events that ultimately led us to this track we're on together right now. We best get to it.

With all three children well into their school years, one about to graduate soon, mounting expenses related to building a home and all that goes with it, in addition to a marriage in crisis, Mom returned to work. She took a job at Rawlings, a local baseball and baseball bat factory in town. Dad often traveled for work with the roofing contractor and eventually his own construction company. I babysat my brothers while Mom and Dad worked and traveled. Greg and

Jimmy had grown to an age where they really didn't need a babysitter. They were old enough to tend to themselves yet required at least a young adult's supervision. The boys had taken an interest in BMX bikes. Most days, they rode their bikes into town where they had makeshift ramps and gadgets set up in a parking lot for customers of the local pharmacy, bank, laundromat, and pizza parlor. They free-styled up and down the ramps they had constructed while spinning the handlebars on their bikes. They jumped from ramp to ramp and landed two wheels with perfection on the asphalt parking lot. They didn't stop short with bike stunts. This led to interest in skateboarding. Soon enough, the plywood ramps they built were frequented by Greg, Jimmy, and all their crew on skateboards rather than bikes. In fact, it became their primary source of transportation as they skateboarded through town, from business to business, and to and from school. Their school was positioned atop a large hill, which made for a perfect incline leaving school each day where they could gain speed and momentum on their colorful skateboards.

During the winter months in Upstate New York when snow and ice didn't allow for ideal weather conditions to ride BMX bikes or skateboards, the boys gained interest in a different kind of board, minus the wheels. There was a ski slope not far from our hometown called Shumaker Mountain. Greg and Jimmy took an interest in snowboarding there. My brothers frequented the slopes as often as they could. Eventually, Mom and Dad purchased them passes for Christmas to glide down the mountain slopes as often as they desired. They excelled in the sport as they did most anything they pursued in outdoor activities and athletics. They eventually excelled beyond expectations in the sport they loved most, football. But it wasn't quite their time just yet.

There was one matter of attention that—or might I say, who—took Greg's attention from sports. Her name was Julie Schuyler. Julie was one of the most beautiful girls Greg ever had the opportunity to meet at the ripe age of thirteen. She had long, dark-brown to nearly black, curly hair, which was very much the style in 1988. She was slender, with an hourglass shape and had dark-brown eyes that sparkled in the sunlight. She was new to DCS. They were both in seventh grade. She was twelve; he was a year and two days older. Julie quickly became the object of Greg's affection. His goal was clear, he was going to make this new girl in school his girlfriend. After getting to know one another a bit, Greg wrote Julie a letter that fall to ask her if she would be his girl. It was a Friday, and Julie didn't give him an answer to his proposal until Monday. To his excitement, Julie said yes. He invited her to a family picnic at a nearby park soon thereafter, and the two were officially a couple. This was definitely a relationship that would leave a footprint on both of their young hearts.

9

Everything I Do, I Do It for You

Let all that you do be done in love.
—1 Corinthians 16:14 (ESV)

Brother found love. Greg and Julie's bond progressed into a six-year relationship. This was the first significant relationship either of them had ever experienced. They were young, in love, and the epitome of high school sweethearts. They were a recognizable couple in the halls of their school and around town where they both hung out together often. They frequented the Little League baseball park in town. Greg played baseball there, beginning with T-ball at around five years old all the way up through his early teen years. He predominantly played the positions of pitcher and catcher. In fact, he even made all-state catcher at some point down the road. However, he covered the positions first baseman and shortstop when needed. Julie and her friends frequented the baseball field, sitting on the bleachers with our family while Greg played or at the concession stand purchasing snacks.

Eventually, Greg took interest in football. It was an unspoken family tradition that every man in the Foster family would play the popular sport in this particular hometown, which wasn't a burden since he loved the game anyway. He began playing football on the junior varsity modified team, and Julie watched on the sidelines or on the bleachers, much in the same way that she did at his baseball games. After all, he was one to be watched. He had recognizable talent as the fullback on the football field at that time. His coaches, Mr. Mahardy and Mr. Mueller, certainly took notice. I'm sure they reported back to Coach Walczak. He was the one to impress. Coach Walczak had been around for quite some time. In fact, he was our father's football coach over twenty-five years earlier. He was well-known throughout the entire region for his coaching ability and expertise. We'll talk more about him a little later.

Back to Greg and Julie. They were practically inseparable. Where one was, the other was usually in the immediate vicinity. When they weren't in the halls or at their lockers together during the school days, on the baseball and football fields after school, or even at the parking lot where Greg and his friends gathered with their skateboards, they could be found together during other activities such as band. Greg played the drums, an understatement, to say the least. Julie was on the color guard team in the marching band. Brother had been drumming most of his life. As a toddler and very young child, he drummed constantly on anything that could be drummed on with his bare hands, pencils, or eating utensils. He was often scolded for drumming on the table during dinner, on his desk during school, and even on the passenger seats in the vehicle as Mom and Dad were driving. Our parents finally realized that it was undeniable; drumming was part of who he was and bought him his first toy drum set when he was about five years old. When he was thirteen years old, he joined the junior high band at school and started taking professional lessons with his band teacher. His instructor gave him a drum block to practice on at home and he did so often until that following Christmas of 1987. He made his heart's desire well-known that he only wanted one thing for Christmas that year and one thing alone. He wanted a drum set. A drum set was not a cheap purchase at that time, especially for our parents who were struggling to make ends meet and with another preteen and teenager in the household to buy for. Somehow, someway, Mom and Dad made it work. Brother woke up on Christmas morning in 1987 to a shiny black-and-silver CB-700 international drum set.

It was by far the best gift he had ever received, at least in his eyes. Our household was seldom silent again as he drummed from the time he got off the school bus each day until he went to bed each night. He drummed for anyone who would listen as he absolutely wore out the base, snare, toms, high hats, and cymbals. There were two audience members who didn't seem to mind him entertaining them with the beat of his drums. Nick and Nat were two of our many first cousins on Dad's side of the family. Their father Gary, Dad's brother, had been killed in a motorcycle accident when the boys were very young. They came over from time to time and listened to Greg as he put on a show for them pounding on the heads of the drums for hours. It was the generation of hard rock and heavy metal music, and Greg loved nothing more than to turn on his stereo and play along to Metallica, Guns N' Roses, Aerosmith, Dave Matthews Band, Led Zeplin, Queen, and other rock groups popular in the eighties and nineties. It was no secret that his mom didn't prefer his choice in music. He wasn't being disrespectful. He just genuinely enjoyed listening to and playing his drums along with his favorite hard rock and heavy metal bands. To each his own, as they say.

Although Greg had struggled with reading and academics most of his grade school years, even repeating the first grade because of dyslexia and the effects it had on his reading ability, he excelled in everything he put his hands to in the areas of athletics, art, and music. He was all heart, and when he was passionate about something, he pursued it with every fiber of his being. Combined with his creative and artistic personality and natural gifts, his passion drove him to excel in sports, drums, and arts. He loved hard and he hurt hard. In the right circumstances, being all heart helped him, but sometimes it caused hardship for him because he fought for what and who he loved, even physically if he deemed necessary. That's just sort of how boys worked things out back in those days when disagreements could be resolved by duking it out free of criminal charges and lawsuits. Brother definitely fell into that category. He was known to fight, often, usually not because of a personal offense, but quite often defending someone he loved or merely sticking up for the underdog. He didn't have much tolerance of anyone making fun of a peer with a disability or underprivileged via socioeconomic status. He was equally intolerant of anyone who would choose to be abusive or inhumane to an animal. He had even less tolerance to anyone badmouthing a member of his family, whether immediate or distant relative. If you happened to find yourself on the receiving end of that unfortunate event, you would come to associate specific statements with the sting of pain. In the same vein, however, he was the type of person who would not hesitate to put someone to the ground who found themselves in any category of intolerance on his personal Richter scale but was equally known for extending a hand when it was all said and done and his opponent had fallen into submission to help the defeated foe back up to his feet. Sometimes they would even shake hands and begin a newfound friendship once an understanding had been reached as to what would be acceptable behavior and what would not. Other times, an agreement was unspoken yet understood to agree to disagree. For most, one brief encounter was more than they ever desired to endure ever again in their entire lifetime. For others still, especially from neighboring football team rivals, Greg's reputation for being an unofficially official undefeated town brawler, created a scenario where he was challenged to a fight just so that the challenging opponent could add defeating the champion as a notch on their belt, which typically didn't turn out as they planned. This street fighter's wrath fell hard on the sorry soul who harassed, talked unfavorably about or even talked too favorably about his beloved Julie. There isn't anything he wouldn't do for her. He loved her and would fight defending and protecting her.

The popular love song on the radio in the early 1990s was "Everything I Do, I Do It for You" by Bryan Adams. Greg and Julie quickly claimed the popular love song often used as the theme at high school proms as their very own love song. Greg often sang it to Julie every time it played on the radio. For him, the words were literal. He meant every single lyric from the bottom of his young heart, which loved so deeply for his brown-eyed brunette girl he adored. He often told his family he was going to marry her one day. He meant it as much as he meant the lyrics of the song he often sang to his young love.

(Everything I Do) I Do It for You
Bryan Adams

Look into my eyes
You will see
What you mean to me
Search your heart, search your soul
When you find me there, you'll search no more
Don't tell me it's not worth trying for
You can't tell me it's not worth dying for
You know it's true
Everything I do, I do it for you

Look into your heart, you will find
There's nothing there to hide
Take me as I am, take my life
I would give it all, I would sacrifice
Don't tell me it's not worth fighting for
I can't help it, there's nothing I want more
You know it's true
Everything I do, I do it for you

There is no love like your love
And no other could give me more love
There's nowhere unless you're there
All the time, all the way

You can't tell me it's not worth trying for
Just can't help it, there's nothing I want more
I would fight for you
Yeah, I'd lie for you
Walk the wire for you
Yeah, I'd die for you
You know it's true
Everything I do, I do it for you

Songwriters: Bryan Adams, John Lange, and Michael Kamen

10

The Fall

For all have sinned and fall short of the glory of God.
                                        —Romans 3:23 (NASB)

Just as sand flows through the hourglass of life, the hands of a clock continue rotating, and the pages of a calendar are turned, Greg passed the torch of junior high to his little brother Jimmy. The moment had arrived.

All elementary and junior high milestones would lead to the occasion we all anxiously await. Bittersweet on that final day, we, alongside our classmates we have grown up with for the last thirteen developmental years of our lives, march down the aisles of the auditorium to pomp and circumstance. Considered an adult for the very first time in our lives as childhood vanishes in a respectable handshake with the authority and leader of the place we have spent eight-hour days (Mondays through Fridays) for thirteen years to exchange the scroll-like document called a diploma. Hundreds of doting friends and family members gather in the space where every momentous occasion throughout the course of our entire youths has been celebrated to observe and honor those draped in robes and adorned in caps and gowns representative of the coveted school colors glide across the stage where the sound of dress shoes click against hardwood floors. We had come to the long-awaited commencement ceremony when the tassels of the flat, square lid, affixed to our tresses and secured with bobby pins, are turned from one side to the other, creating a sense of finality. Bittersweet emotions of joy, sadness, fear, and anticipation of the future create a cosmic collision in the depths of our souls. Nonetheless, this is the journey called life.

It was time for my brother Greg to join me in walking the speckled, ceramic-tile floors of the long, narrow, and locker-lined hallways of the James A. Green High School. I would only be fortunate enough to cross paths with Greg in the upper classmen halls for one year as it was my senior year when he entered ninth grade. It was 1990, the year I graduated and passed my own high school legacy to my middle brother to look after the baby of the family, Jimmy who was in seventh grade. It was a sobering reality, reflecting on this season of life. It was time to empty the nest that had been very much built with slivered sticks on a rocky foundation, take my broken wings, and learn to fly in the frailty of my own shattered dreams. I looked forward to the day that eventually comes for all of us if we're so fortunate. Regardless of how much or how little we are prepared for it, it isn't always easy to pull shards of broken glass from blood-filled arteries. Yet familiarity is often the comfort zone and safety net we learn to depend on from the time of infancy. I yearned to understand codependency, a state of being I had heard about yet couldn't grasp due to youth, developmental immaturity, spiritual wandering, and the denial of naivety.

How could I abandon these two boys, my biological brothers but seemed like my own children I had mothered, protected, cared for, and took under my wing for seventeen long years? They were growing up and somehow relying on me much less than they used to. Perhaps God was preparing us to live independently from one another. The only resemblance of life I would leave with them would be the stray dogs I had brought home and manipulated my parents into making official members of our family. The bright-red bows I tied around their necks I'm sure did not hurt my case after finding the pups wandering like lost sheep around town. Still dressed in the blue-and-white band uniform I wore to the football games where I played a black clarinet for four years, I prepared an effective defense. It was how Virgil, the reddish-orange cocker spaniel, and Hogan, the short-legged mixture of a lot of various breeds, were welcomed as four-legged members of the Foster kinfolk.

Looking beyond the inner turmoil and clashing of all that I was leaving behind, I was excited for the next chapter in my life. I had been dating my high school sweetheart since the end of my sophomore year in 1988. Two years older than me, he was a senior and graduating a month later in June. He had already been accepted and received a football scholarship to attend Ithaca College. It certainly wasn't desirable or ideal at the time, but we decided that we would continue forward in our relationship, although it would be a long-distance one while I finished my final two years of high school. Nobody told us it would be easy. It was every bit as difficult as we had imagined, but we saw one another during his winter, spring, and summer breaks from college when he came home. We didn't have cell phones, text messaging, social media, or even access to the Internet back in 1988. We utilized landline phone calls and wrote each other letters that had to be sent via the United States Postal Service. After enduring a difficult, two-year, long-distance relationship, I graduated from high school in June 1990. We made plans that I would relocate to Ithaca, a three-hour drive from our hometown, where he was attending college and I would enroll in a college in that area. Circumstances don't always work out as we expect. This was to be one of such circumstances in my life. Foiled plans and failed relationships can change the course of our entire lives.

Domestic matters had become very messy on the home front. After many tumultuous years, my mom and dad's marriage of nearly twenty years was officially over. The situation had gone so terribly awry, there was nothing remotely amicable about it. My brothers and I were very much caught up in the eye of a violent storm that raged over our household. I vowed from the beginning of this narrative that my mom and dad's story was their own. It is not my business or appropriate for me to air their dirty laundry to the public. Grandpa Daley always taught us to do unto others as we would want to have done to us. Surely, none of our closets are completely free and clear of any skeletons. However, to the extent that the dissolution of my parents' marriage affected my brothers and me, it is indeed necessary to at least skim over it a bit. I have their permission to do so. After all, one of their three children is soon to become the main character of this story.

Mom moved into an apartment in town. She couldn't afford much, and she was starting over from scratch. Mom and I left the place that was just beginning to feel like home on North Road and moved into a humble, one-bedroom upstairs apartment of a run-down, hunter-green, two-family home in town. We enlisted the benevolent services of Catholic Charities and were blessed to be given some basic, mismatched essentials that included an old second-hand sectional sofa. The sofa served double duty as Mom's bed in the living room that was also her bedroom. She gave me the one small bedroom the apartment had. A square secondhand card table and a few off-white plastic yard chairs were positioned in the center of our outdated kitchen where we ate our meals often received from a local food pantry. Mom cried a lot. She was physically present yet emotionally absent. I struggled with my newfound identity. Life as I once knew it had drastically changed. I became emotionally numb, yet very angry and confused. Fear of the unknown and future wreaked havoc on me physically, emotionally, academically, and relationally. The impact was noticeable as I was plagued with anxiety and depression, and struggled to finish out my senior year of high school, which was reflected in my SAT scores.

Greg stayed in our newly constructed yet unfinished home with Dad. Jimmy lived back and forth between both parents' residences. Separation and divorce are never easy for kids. Likewise, the destruction of our family unit as we knew it was no less difficult for Greg, Jimmy, and me. The three of us had been so close yet now we were all separated after many years. I focused on my relationship and getting through my last year of high school. Jimmy was still young. He hung out with friends and did what middle school boys do, which included tagging along with his big brother, Greg. The two boys were brothers but they were also very much each other's best friends. Experiencing nearly everything together, the two brothers went from being playmates when they were little to riding bikes, skateboarding, and snowboarding as they got a little older. They played sports together and even participated in foolishness together as teenage boys sometimes do, dabbling and experimenting with smoking cigarettes and drinking beer. For instance, they were not much over the age of eleven and thirteen when Dad decided to make a surprise visit to their "camp." The boys had a camp on the Plant for many years. After we relocated to North Road, they needed a new place to call home away from home in the woods. So they took a load of lumber that Dad had delivered to the home that he was in the process of building. They carried the lumber deep into the woods and used it to build a new humble abode. Needless to say, Dad was extremely unhappy with his sons' indiscretions. As time went along, he forgave them, as parents do. When the time came for the boys to have their first official sleepover in their newly constructed camp, there was one foreseen problem.

Greg had been afraid of the dark since he was a small child. He reasoned with dad that part of the reason for his desire to sleep outdoors in the woods was to overcome his fear of the dark. Dad was suspicious of Greg's newfound quest to conquer his fear. After all, the boys' new home was deep in the heart of the woods behind their primary residence. It lacked any source of illumination other than the light of the moon or the big dipper on a starry night, which varied depending on how the planets aligned with one another. There was absolutely no other visible lighting in their neck of the thickets. Surely, if Greg had a longing to overcome his fear of the dark, this would be the ideal—or perhaps, not very ideal—environment to do so. Dad granted their request, however, once it was completely pitch black in the country, Dad snuck down through the brushes and stayed a while, unbeknownst to Greg, Jimmy, and their friend Mike from down the street. Mike arrived with beer he had just stolen from Moore's Market, a small convenience store at the end of North Road, which was also a popular place with the locals to purchase made-to-order pizzas and submarine sandwiches. The three boys were clearly busted, and their punishment was unpleasant. The next day, Dad made them face Grant, the family friend and owner of the market they stole the beer from, to offer an in-person apology. Dad asked for restitution in any manner Grant saw fit. Thankfully, Grant was merciful to the ashamed young boys and claimed that the debt had been satisfied with a mere apology and compensation for what they had taken without further consequence.

Dad kept this secret between them and never told Mom what the boys had done. They weren't exactly on speaking terms at the time. After all, any attempt at the near impossible feat of simple communication between two wounded ex-spouses endeavoring as co-parents to their three children resulted in an intense argument. I believe I have just let the cat out of the bag, so to speak, after all these years regarding the events of that dark summer night at camp. Although I don't know that Mom will ever read this book. I could honestly understand if she didn't. No parent should ever be subjected to the level of pain she or Dad would endure by reading it on black-and-white pages. After all, there is something immensely real in the finality of viewing a painful reality when etched in permanent ink.

Mischief and dabbling did not end there for my brothers. I never claimed that I wore any sort of angelic halo atop my head. I was more interested in breaking the rules and boundaries with my boyfriend and attracted to foolishness and pranks rather than drugs and alcohol. I never experimented or even tried any illicit drugs, however, I dabbled with a little bit of alcohol myself. Only by God's grace did it not end up on the top of my list of troubles. Many years later, my therapist told me that the anecdotes I created and the ability to laugh at my own circumstances were a coping mechanism for me. For the casual observer, it was evident that I was battling some profound anguish due to the nature of my horsing around. I was. Behind a forced smile were the secrets I was keeping buried within the confidentiality of my own heart and mind, bearing a striking resemblance to the skeletons hiding in my parents' closet. It was a familiar place. I've heard it said that history has a unique way of repeating itself. I'm not exactly sure how that manifests in one's life. After all, it's not as if I was looking to clone my parents' marriage and the effects the dissolution of it had on my brothers and me. In fact, I thought I was running as fast as I could in the opposite direction, yet somehow, without warning and hidden beneath the deception of charm, I was leaping headfirst into it.

From time to time on the cloudy or rainy days within the depths of my fractured spirit, I contemplated ending my own life. I thank Grandpa Daley that on those days, which seemed to appear more often than sunshine during that particular season, my thoughts remained a figment of my imagination alone. A means of God's grace and provision in my life, Grandpa said on occasion that from an eternal perspective, it was a profound lack of wisdom to play God. Hence, on any given day, I could be discovered acting foolishly with my aunt Dorothy, who was one of my closest friends and my two other best buddies, Melissa and Colleen. Chasing boys and foolish pranks occupied the wandering space in my teenage heart for the most part. Likely, those factors and the natural fears and anxieties within my soul superseded and provided a barrier of protection against a desire to experiment with what I would have classified as dangerous. Perhaps greater than fear was the control freak mentality I had acquired. I didn't like to not be in control or, worse yet, allow a foreign substance to force me to relinquish what little in my life that I had the ability to control. Years later, a therapist told me that I had adopted a frame of mind that had so little control over the chaotic environment all around me that I overcompensate in the areas of life I *do* have some control over.

It would also be fair to say that my parents were stricter with me than they were with my brothers. There was very much a double standard of sorts that existed within the parenting parameters of our family dynamics. The theory that what was good for the goose was not also good for the gander was enlisted as an understood household rule. I was a girl, after all, and there were dangers far more serious in the world for a female than that of a male. At least, that was the analogy of my father. I didn't understand it or appreciate it back then. I deemed it unfair in the astuteness of my youth. Maybe it was. Regardless, my father's flawed philosophies—or what was my conceptualization of the household rules at the time—likely did me more good than harm in the long run. I would come to bear witness to that fact at some point in the very near future. In the moment, however, it created a source of conflict between my dad and me. I deeply longed for an acceptance and approval from him, which I perceived was nonexistent.

I can't pinpoint the specific moment when I began wrestling with the feeling that somehow I was not enough or identify the cause of my long-term battle with insecurity. Although I was enlightened many years later in therapy about some possible contributing factors, it didn't make any of the resulting damage go away by dwelling on it. It was just there, and I didn't know how to rectify it. So, statistically, I did what the general population of insecure girls do at that age. I sought the approval and affection I craved from any male figure I perceived would fulfill the longing within me, whether genuine, generic, or fabricated for his own gain. My difference in opinions on disciplinary matters with my father and insecurity I contended with pointed to an outward source of a very deep inner conflict within my soul. I was bitter about my parents' divorce and all that had led up to it. I was, in a sense, stuck, unrelenting, and non-resilient in any ability to move forward from the past and ongoing present crisis. Thank the good Lord that time, wisdom and maturity heals all wounds. Becoming a mom myself I suppose contributed much to the capacity to understand when gazing through the parenting lens from a different perspective and role. Looking from the outside into the window of our hearts in the year 2017, an observer would see a very different relationship between a father and his daughter. However, even the best relationships are tested at some point. As a matter of fact, I would venture to say that testing—although unpleasant at the time—was necessary in relationships and in the general theme of life. Trials strengthen, mature, and grow the feeble character, mind, and soul of humanity. I wish we had the right to pick and choose the storms that make landfall in our backyards, but that power wasn't bestowed upon us in the garden of Eden.

Our family was certainly not granted any sovereign immunity of sorts. In fact, we would come to be tested in a profoundly unimaginable way. It wouldn't be long now before it would knock on our front door. If only someone could have warned us. I don't suppose it would have changed the outcome any, although it's effortless at times within the simplicity of our own flawed humanity to believe we are in control. God's will is God's will. That's what Grandpa Daley always said anyway. But how could something so unfathomable be the will of a holy, loving, perfect, and omniscient Father who claims to love His children? I certainly don't fault you for asking such a question. This is not the type of theology that is natural to wrap our warped minds around. In fact, it took me a very long time to grapple this topic out with Almighty God. He was patient with me in His relentless pursuit to help me understand. Some days, I think I do understand it. Other days, well, I guess it's only natural that although we were created to always be moving forward, looking forward, and speaking forward, sometimes our gears get shifted into reverse. When that happens, we have limited choices other than to back up a little, redirect our gaze, and keep moving forward, if that makes any logical sense.

The middle child, my brother Greg, was at a vulnerable age and couldn't quite find his place as our family crumbled all around him. He loved our mother so deeply yet was close to our father and had a sense of loyalty to him. He struggled intensely within the emotions and entanglement of feeling stuck in the middle, torn between both parents and siblings he loved so much. He continued in his relationship with Julie. The two broke up and got back together often throughout their six-year relationship from seventh grade all the way through to twelfth grade. Some breakups were longer than others, and during some of their time apart, they even dated other people. In due time, they always found their way back to each other. They did all the things high school sweethearts do. They were usually at one another's homes when school and football practice was over each day. Just being together, not doing anything special outside of lounging on the couch and just watching TV together, was special to them. Occasionally, they hung out together with friends at the community youth center where they played an occasional game of pool. The pair also enjoyed the neighborhood roller skating rink where they held hands and skated under revolving colored lights to popular early nineties hits by Tiffany, All-4-One, Whitney Houston, and Mariah Carey. Together with the large group of friends they often hung out with, they gathered to go bowling at the local bowling alley. When all else failed, there was usually a back road party on Winkler or Carlson Roads and at Boyer's Pit, where masses of teens and young adults congregated for a night of drinking and shenanigans. They mutually attended school functions, events, and dances. Of course, there was the big school dance, the dance of all dances—prom. Like most of the other prom attendees, they rented out a limo, went out for dinner, paraded around the school for pictures in their prom dress and tuxedo, danced, and made memories.

Greg also continued immersing himself in sports (namely, football), art class, and drumming. He excelled in all three. However, where he shined the brightest was on the football field. Playing from the time he was in junior high all the way to high school, he gained the attention of the high school football coach, Coach Walczak. Coach Walczak was the one to impress. He had been my dad's high school football coach and was well-known throughout the region, winning numerous awards at both local and national levels for his exceptional coaching abilities. The award-winning coach took notice of not only Greg's extraordinary aptitudes, but his passion and heart for the game as well. Greg made the first string of the high school football team in tenth grade, which was not the standard protocol. He played the position of middle linebacker. If you're anything like me and don't understand all that's entailed in the game of football, that would be the guy in the center of the field calling the defensive plays, reminiscent of the quarterback for the defense. Most of us not versed in the terminology of the all-American sport at least recognize the title of quarterback enough to realize that it's a vital role for any team.

Speaking of the quarterback, it was Brian Lasowski during Greg's high school football career. Brian and Greg had been very good friends since they were young boys. They had gone to school together since kindergarten and played sports together beginning with T-ball. It was how our two families met and became close friends. My dad was the president of the Little League and head coach of the team my brothers played on. Brian's father Ron was elected vice president of the league and functioned as one of dad's assistant coaches.

As a result, our families became good friends both on the baseball field and off. Mom and Dad often went to Ron and Bonnie Lasowski's home, not far from the baseball field, after games for dinner, cookouts, and cards. Greg, Jimmy and Brian all played together, while Brian's younger sister Kristin and I frolicked around together. The friendship continued all the way through Little League years. Although our families remained friendly as our household unit dissolved, our relationships were affected. As the nature of the two families' affiliation with one another was altered, the children's connection followed suit. The boys didn't hang out together as often, mainly because the parents didn't fraternize any longer. Greg met some new friends through skateboarding. We'll talk about them shortly. They are a huge part of this story. However, as of right now, we are just leaving the Little League Park and making our way to the high school football field.

Greg and Brian had a close relationship on the football field. Both had been elected by the team as cocaptains, a high honor. They worked closely together to lead the team of the game they both loved so deeply. Greg chose the number 25 as his jersey number in eighth grade junior varsity modified football. It had been our father's football number, and he wanted to carry it on. He did so very well. Greg was a member of the 1993 Blue Devils whose team had moved up from class D to class C. The team finished 10–0 with a league championship and the school's first Section III championship in class C. Julie wore her boyfriend's jersey at school as well as on the bleachers on game day, which read "Foster" at the top back of the jersey with the number 25 on both the front and back. That's just what high school sweethearts did back in the 1990s in the small, close-knit high school known for their undefeated football record. Greg's high school football team's record was 30–0. From the tenth through twelfth grade, they played and won thirty games, losing none. They were undefeated champions in the entire region amongst schools in their class. Brother was an incredibly aggressive athlete. He was all heart, had a passion for the game and a will to win. In fact, he didn't acknowledge losing as an acceptable outcome, which served him and his team well since they never did lose a single game during all three years of Greg's high school football tenure. Even in his entire football career from JV through high school, he and his team only lost a grand total of two games ever, and neither of those were at the high school level.

There was no denying that Greg had an unparalleled skill level and knowledge of the game he so deeply treasured. However, what made him even more extraordinary on the field of touchdowns was his devotion and passion for the game. He was all heart when he played. He and his team were expected to win by their coach, their families, and the hometown that faithfully followed. Losing was not a realistic option. Greg did not take his leadership role as captain of the team lightly. He was as loyal to his teammates as he was to his family. The central anchor point in any good defense, Greg took his position seriously. As a middle linebacker, he was, quite literally, in the center of all things that happen on defense. Tasked with stopping the run, coverage, and normally locked up man-to-man with the running backs out of the backfield or tight ends, he knew what he had to do. Involved in most tackles on defense, his job was to either instigate the initial contact or assist with the defensive play.

Most middle linebackers are generally big, strong, and hard-nosed. The average NFL linebacker is over six foot two inches tall and weighs nearly two hundred thirty pounds. Weighing in at about a hundred eighty pounds on his five foot ten frame, Greg was average in stature, height, and weight. At first glance, he was not a teenage boy that one would consider larger than the norm. However, he certainly was not small or puny. He was average in overall size for a male of his age. Don't get me wrong. He enjoyed working out, weight lifting, and training in the gym in between football practices. He had an athletic, lean, and muscular body type. Although he had a nice build, it wasn't necessarily his size that created the perfect formulation for a quality player. A middle linebacker must be strong and able to be a physical tackler play after play. The position is not for someone who shies away from contact. Quick, strong and involved in almost every play, he must be a player who likes to hit and can bring down the best running backs out there. The goal of the linebacker is clear, to provide either extra run protection or extra pass protection based on the defensive play being executed. Linebackers are often regarded as the most important position in defense, due to their versatility in providing hard hits on running plays or an additional layer of pass protection when required. Linebackers are required to use their judgment on every snap to determine their role during any particular given play.

My brother Greg was the epitome of a top-notch middle linebacker because of his heart, personality, drive, loyalty, the natural-born protector in him, and the fact that he wasn't afraid to face his giants. He wasn't afraid to take risks regardless of the cost. He was quick and a bit impulsive, battling some deep-rooted inner pain that he carried with him on the field. A key vocal leader and communicator for all the linebackers and defensive linemen, he had a duty to call out formation strength, signals, and adjustments. His alignment on the field he cherished allowed him to step quickly to the left or right to fill gaps and stop the run. His assignment was to be the primary gap destroyer and run stopper. He proudly took on any lead blocks and spilled the back to his teammates if need be. In the case of a pass, Greg dropped to his appropriate responsibility, depending on the coverage called. He also had a sense of humor. As a key vocal leader and team captain, he enjoyed using his position of authority to make the song selections for the pregame introduction. This was the point and time just before the game started. The two teams were introduced over the loudspeaker and ran out on the field, usually to a thematic song that best represented their team and served the purpose of rousing both the teams and spectators. A classmate and lifelong friend of Brother's (I believe he actually had a bit of a crush on her in their elementary years), Katie Potts, was in charge of the music for home games. Greg had a habit of making a special request on behalf of the opposing team. He requested a masculine, warrior song, such as "Eye of the Tiger" from the *Rocky III* soundtrack, for the Dolgeville Blue Devil players to rush the field from the locker rooms. But he got a chuckle out of having classical instrumentals, such as "Flight of the Bumblebee" and "Hungarian Dances," playing as the opposing team entered the field.

He fought hard for his teammates and the spectators who had become dependent on a win for their hometown team they represented with so much pride. Sometimes he fought literally. He was a scrapper both on and off the field if he or someone he cared about was wronged in some way. Sometimes to a fault. Regretting the consequence after the fact, he was distraught during the Clinton game that fall of 1993. Clinton was not a school that had classified as the Blue Devil's arch rival. That was West Canada Valley High School. However, it was a team that qualified as a runner-up. Greg would not have been thrilled about sitting on the bench during any game where his teammates were on the field. It was his job to be out there to serve and protect. However, sitting the bench during games with some opponents was a greater sting than others. This was one of those occasions. In the game leading up to this one, the kid on the opposing team who was in a rage over the fact that Greg just tackled him, probably was deserving of the whooping he took on the field. I might venture to say any of us may have reacted the same way my brother did. He was merely doing his job. No one enjoys an uppercut under the helmet whilst otherwise should be celebrating a gain on the scoreboard. After all, there were a group of attractive high school girls dressed in pleated, blue-and-white miniskirts on the sidelines, waving matching-colored pom-poms and shouting, "Go Blue! Go White! Go Team! Fight, fight!" Just behind the cheerleaders on the bleachers, the pep band chanted, "Go Big Blue!" as the fans clapped and shouted along. He was robbed of his moment to shine.

Although Coach Walczak cringed at the thought of benching one of his key players who had been officially named MVP of multiple games, an example had to be made, a threat had to be followed through, and a lesson must be learned. Thankfully for the team who depended upon his participation and Greg's pride, Coach Walczak only needed to resort to that type of outcome on that one occasion. Greg was great at defense and diversified in offense, both passing and running the ball. He was excellent at special teams and a gifted all-around ballplayer. The reward for competing at an undefeated level was the goal each year, which was participating at the sectional championship level at the Carrier Dome at Syracuse University in Syracuse, New York. In fact, Greg had the great honor of playing there for the championship title multiple times, taking home the section D championship title on each occasion. Coach Walczak thought highly of and cared deeply for Brother. He recognized the talent and passion Greg had and his importance to the team. Coach Walczak often utilized football tapes highlighting Greg's plays at future practices. He often commented, "Greg and Jimmy Foster are two of the best middle linebackers this school has ever had."

Speaking of my brother Jimmy, it wasn't long before he joined the ranks on the football field alongside our brother. Following in his older brother's footsteps, Jimmy made the high school team as a sophomore after playing junior varsity modified football during eighth and ninth grades. When Jimmy joined the high school team as a sophomore, Greg was a senior. Jimmy wore the jersey number 23 and played alongside Greg as the weak side linebacker during his sophomore year, eventually replacing Greg as the middle linebacker during his junior and senior years. Jimmy played varsity football from 1993–1995, playing alongside his brother Greg from 1993–1994. Together on the field, Greg playing the middle linebacker position and Jimmy right at his side as the weak side linebacker, the two brothers were a force to be reckoned with. With their team, they amassed a three-year overall record of twenty-nine wins against only two losses. Both of those losses were at the state competition level. They did win three consecutive league and sectional championships.

Eventually, after Greg's high school football career came to an end, Jimmy stepped in and carried on our brother's title as middle linebacker. Following in the footsteps of Greg was no simple feat and certainly not painless cleats to fill. After all, being the younger brother in the shadow of an older brother who was a football star wasn't easy. Jimmy was named Most Valuable Defensive Player in the Section III Finals, along with being named All-League and All-State in 1995. With all team records that had been accomplished during Jimmy's three varsity years, there was a specific game in which

Jimmy had one of his most outstanding highlights. In the game versus Sauquoit on September 30, 1995, when Dolgeville was then ranked number one in the state in class C, Jimmy lead the defense to a team victory by a score of 25–12. His accomplishments on that unprecedented day included five tackles, one fumble recovery, and one interception. In the Notre Dame game on October 13, 1995, Jimmy recorded a team leading eleven tackles in that victory by the Blue Devils by a score of 35–7. Another notable mention was the class C regional game where Dolgeville was ranked number one and its opponent, Delhi, was ranked number two in the state. Jimmy was named the game's most valuable player with thirteen tackles in Dolgeville's win by a score of 7–6. This win would move the Blue Devils to its first appearance in the state semifinals. Although the Blue Devils were defeated in that game, Jimmy completed his high school football career on a team that delivered fifty consecutive wins against Section III opponents.

Like Greg, there was no doubt that Jimmy shared an equivalent love and passion for the game of football. Much like his big brother whom he looked up to immensely, his knowledge and skill level was unparalleled. Sadly, the similarities didn't stop short at talent and fervor. Just as his older siblings were battling their own inner brokenness, Jimmy was not immune from turmoil within, resulting from all that was happening in his family life. Like Greg, he carried deep emotion with him on the football field and on the wrestling mats as he eventually became a wrestler, holding the class D title during off season as a middle linebacker. Jimmy would soon play the game he loved with a different mind-set. He knew he had very large shoes to fill as he changed position from outside linebacker to middle linebacker, his older brother's position. Knowing that Greg was amazing, Jimmy felt a need to represent him well and make him proud. Playing with all of Greg's craziness and passion, Jimmy sought the approval of not only his coach, teammates, fans, friends, and family, but most of all, his older brother who had gone before him and paved the way. This wouldn't be the only time Greg would pave the way, not only for Jimmy, but also for me and many others. This was only the beginning.

11

Slow Fade

Above all else, guard your heart, for everything you do flows from it.
—Proverbs 4:23 (NIV)

Looking back in the rearview mirror of life, the tackles and touchdowns may have been a provision and means of grace and mercy at the very hand of God Himself for my two brothers. For me, Almighty Father was indeed still very much at work. We were going through so much at home with our parents' marriage crumbling and the bitter divorce and custody battle that followed. For the first time ever, we were all living separate lives. We didn't attend church much anymore after we left the Plant where we didn't have much of an excuse not to since the church was directly across the street from our home.

The good Lord did bless me with a very good friend. Her name was Lee. We had gone to school together most of our lives. She lived just one road up from our home on North Road, much deeper into the forest of pine trees and swarms of blackflies and mosquitos. We spent a lot of time together at her house, which was shaped like a barn. It was difficult to have friends over at our residence during that time in our lives. Lee came from a very strong family of faith. I attended church with her and her family from time to time. Every Wednesday evening, her relatives and various members of their church gathered at Lee's aunt's home for a prayer meeting. Aunt Janet was middle-aged at that time. She was petite in size yet mighty in faith.

I attended the Pentecostal gatherings with Lee's family on a regular basis. We spent long hours, often until late at night, singing praise and worship songs, studying scripture, and deep in prayer. At times, the elders of the church babbled a language that I didn't understand, yet I had a sense deep within my soul that whatever it was, it was moving and powerful. They always said they were being baptized in the Holy Spirit. Although it was unusual, sometimes it would move me to multilayered emotions and deep waters that I believe God was using to bring healing from cavernous scars.

When I was sixteen years old, Lee's family invited me to attend a large youth conference in Boston, Massachusetts. I'm grateful to this very day that I went as it was an amazing experience. I didn't understand a great deal at that time, but I recognized some of what I had learned there. It was familiar. Grandpa Daley had talked about that kind of stuff since I was an infant. I knew that although I didn't fully understand, whatever it was that I experienced there at that conference, almost as if something greater and outside of myself, it was life transformational. Something was different inside of my spirit. The pastor said I received Jesus into my heart and that His finished work on the cross cancelled out all my sin and shortcomings. He said that I had been made new. The old was gone, and I had been reborn and in a sense given a clean slate. Lord knows I needed a brand-new whiteboard. My old one was so messy with the graffiti of life's circumstances, it was hard to see clearly what was deep beneath the surface masked by chaos. My only regret was that my brothers weren't there with me to experience what I just had. It was something I wanted to share with everyone I cared about. Well, that's not entirely the truth. I had two very specific regrets. The first was that my brothers weren't there with me to experience what I just had right alongside me. The second was that I allowed a greater power in my life at that time, my boyfriend, to pull me away from what I knew to be true. It wasn't that he didn't believe in God. But what the pastor at the youth conference I had just returned from said was that *believing* in God was not enough. He said that the only way to the Father (God) was through the Son (Jesus), and that the only way we could truly be in right relationship with our heavenly Father was through an acceptance of Jesus as our personal Lord and Savior and subsequent life-transforming relationship with Him.

My boyfriend had been raised in an Italian Catholic family, and they occasionally attended mass. I attended with them sometimes. So they believed, but I never really understood to what extent. It wasn't clearly evident on the outside flesh as to what was going on inside of the heart. They were good people with good morals. They were professionals, financially secure, had a nice home, were well-respected in the community, and believed family was important. They weren't criminals. I spent a good amount of time with them, but I don't know that I would have recognized a manifestation of a relationship with Jesus other than the fact that they attended mass. It was sort of a family tradition. Since I spent a lot of time in their home when things had become very messy at my own house, I moved in with them for a few months during my senior year. My boyfriend was off at college so his parents took me in and allowed me to stay in his bedroom while he was away. I was very good friends with his younger sister at the time so it worked.

As for my salvation experience at the youth camp, my boyfriend wasn't excited as I thought he would be to hear my news. Maybe it was his own lack of understanding that made him tell me I had joined a cult. He wasn't much into allowing Jesus to take control over our lives and living for Christ. Faith to him was something he thought of as almost inherited from parents and grandparents. Going to the beautiful stone building on the corner of the four-way stop in town for Saturday evening or Sunday morning mass was a family tradition. Going to mass as a family was considered much in the same way as they celebrated with "sauce," as his grandmother called it, which was an Italian pasta dinner every Sunday afternoon. In a sense, their theology was works-based. I had tried working hard to be good and do the right things on my own but failed miserably. No matter how much I *did* or how hard I worked to earn the love, acceptance, and favor of my heavenly Father, somehow I always fell short. I couldn't ever measure up or get it right enough to be worthy of His affection or approval of me. It felt too much like what I had already experienced in every botched area of my life, whether at home, at school, or in relationships. Nonetheless, it wasn't long after returning home from that life-changing conference in Boston before I gradually faded back into my old habits, lifestyle, and familiarities, not that I was a criminal or out doing horrific things. I guess I was a "good" person. Good according to what though? Who is the judge that sets the scale for a particular level of *goodness*? If I were going to live according to the standards set forth in the Ten Commandments, I would absolutely fail, which I suppose is the precise reason I needed a savior, someone who would exchange their righteousness and holiness for my flaws and shortcomings.

In the meantime, just as I allowed my high school sweetheart to determine the path I would follow in my life's journey, my brothers equally searched for peace, unconditional love, acceptance, approval, and relief from feelings of torment buried deep within their aching souls in other popular places. For them—and more specifically, for Greg—dabbling with drinking and smoking marijuana went from experimentation to full-blown submersion. Unfortunately for the baby of the family, Jimmy, who looked up to his big brother as a role model and aspired to be just like him so much, followed closely behind Greg's footprints.

It's not that I'm attempting to divert the attention from my own shortcomings to the woes of Brother or take the focus off my own life that was spiraling out of control. That's another memoir for another publication. This book isn't about me, nor am I the main character. I am merely the narrator. I apologize in advance that I subjected you to nine long chapters up to this point to get to the main character of this novel. As I reflected back at the beginning of our journey together from tragedy to triumph, I felt like it was important that you not only be able to connect the dots of the story, but also that you connect emotionally to the main character of this story. Just in case you have not yet drawn your own conclusion as to who this story is about, let us take a real sharp turn to right about 1992. We've waited a long time to get here. I believe on some sort of subconscious level, I may have done so intentionally. After all, we are about to dive into the very deep waters. I never wanted to revisit the absolute darkest moment of my life. I'm sure that some of you reading along on this journey with me can relate. Like the Titanic, some of you may have even been in our very ship with us as we treaded deep waters on the exact voyage that sank our vessel. For others still, well, we've all been through something and can relate on various levels. You may need to devote some additional time and space in your physical and emotional environments for these next few chapters. It's going to be an intense expedition to victory. It's time.

I'm not exactly sure just how or when the path of life became blurry. Looking back through the perspective of Monday morning quarterback, there were likely defining moments and identifying factors. It just was. Like a slow fade, the periphery lines of black and white eventually became gray. I suppose it was clear to outsiders peering into the shattered glass of Brother's heart that he was wading in deep waters. It wasn't as if one needed a magnifying glass to see what was evident from the inside out. Perhaps it was the long, black trench coat he and his best friend Gerald wore as they roamed the streets around the town that revealed the darkness raging absolute war on the depths of his fragile soul. Behind his increasingly often bloodshot eyes, those who knew him intimately could almost visibly see the pain he battled. Oddly enough, proximity has a unique way of bonding those going through similar circumstances together. Maybe that was the common thread that tied the five or so boys together into their own unique clique. They all seemingly were going through similar circumstances in one way or another. In a sense, Greg had two separate sets of friends. He was friends with the jocks, the athletes on the football field. But he also had his skateboarding buddies who were essentially like brothers to him. Greg, Gerald, Sean, Richie, and Jim made up the core group alongside our youngest brother Jimmy. Never far away was Julie. She was at the center of Greg's universe, thus central to his closest relationships. Julie had become like a big sister to Jimmy in my absence. By this time, I was a mother to a little boy. My high school sweetheart and I followed through with plans to get an apartment together after I graduated in Ithaca where we both attended college. So I had been about a three-hour drive away from my family for about a year. When my relationship quickly fell apart and I moved back home, I was nineteen, single, and pregnant with my son Zachary. However, moving myself and my baby into what was my dad and brother's bachelor pad didn't go as smoothly as any of us had hoped.

The boys were always together. They enjoyed the simple things in life, like hanging out at camp, backroad parties, bonfires, and house parties; fishing; skateboarding; snowboarding, and riding four wheelers. On any given night, the group could likely be found at the Pizza Lab, the local mom-and-pops style restaurant most popularly known for their New York-style pizza. Some ordered take out. For others, there were tables covered with the traditional checkered red-and-white vinyl tablecloths. In the far rear of the building, there was an area popular with the teenagers in the village. It was filled with brightly colored arcade games complete with a large pool table in the center of the gaming area of the restaurant. Greg and his friends congregated there often, playing Pacman, Super Mario Brothers, Donkey Kong, and other popular 1990s video games until late hours. They spent as much time hanging out in a lot on Main Street in front of the restaurant, which essentially became their boxing ring on any given Saturday night. Times were different then. Throwing punches was an acceptable means of dispute resolution back in those days. When rivals from other towns and schools crossed the border into our little village, they were open game if they chose to speak ill against our town, school, football team, family members, or anyone within the brotherhood that did not resonate well with my brothers or their friends. Julie was an attractive girl. Boys being boys along with puberty and raging hormones, would make catcalls in her direction. That sort of conduct would get them in the Pizza Lab fight zone.

As Greg's reputation for being a town brawler spread throughout the region, he was often challenged to fights in other towns by other reigning champions on their own turfs. It was considered a major victory should any combatant in other municipalities take on another town's scrapper on back roads or at houses parities, local shopping center parking lots, and the like. One of such arch enemies was Jimmer Watson. Jimmer was a brawler from a neighboring city. He and Greg knew one another from run-ins at mutual parties. He provoked Greg often at parties. It was considered a challenge to tussle with another known fighter from a neighboring community so Jimmer often challenged Greg to a fight. Greg resisted the dare on a regular basis. As much as he had the ability to defeat any opponent (in fact, he never lost a fight), he also endeavored to steer clear of them unless he absolutely had no choice. He was quiet, introverted and kept to himself unless he was otherwise provoked. All in all, he sought peace. He enjoyed spending time with Julie and his buddies drinking, smoking marijuana, and just chilling. However, Jimmer committed the ultimate sin. He attempted to sweep Julie off her feet, out of Greg's arms and into his own. Thus an all-out, no-holds-barred war officially ensued between the two boys. After months of taunting, Greg accepted Jimmer's challenge. Greg fretted about this moment for quite some time. Dad didn't advise my brothers that fighting was always the answer. However, he did instruct Greg that should he ever end up in a bad situation with this particular boy who tormented him for so long, he should never go into any fight expecting to lose. Dad told him to face his fears head on. I suppose that's why he called Dad intoxicated at four in the morning shortly thereafter. Dad answered apprehensively due to the hour. "I did it, Dad! I just kicked Jimmer Watson's ass!"

Since the ongoing dispute between Greg and Jimmer had been resolved, he could move on to regular daily life. He worked at Ruggerio's, a nearby Italian restaurant, as a busboy in the evenings after school and on weekends. During summer break from school, he worked in construction with Dad every summer from the time he was fifteen years old. He loved construction. Dad had worked in construction for many years as a roofer and eventually owned his own construction company. Greg very much mimicked anything our father did, and he enjoyed going to work with Dad. As he visited various job sites with Dad, he became fond of the building industry. Dad taught him anything he wanted to know. Much like sports, art, and music, constructing anything with his hands was a natural gift as he was very creative. As he discovered talent, his love of the process increased.

He was saving up for his own car now that he had his driver's license. In the meantime, Dad had to drive him back and forth to work each shift. If Dad didn't need it, he would let Greg use his 1992 burgundy Chevrolet Corsica. The Corsica was brand new at the time; that is, until Brother got ahold of it. He broke it in a bit, so much so that the car had a reputation of its own. Greg, Jimmy, and all their friends who used to pile up inside of it called it the Red Rocket and Old Red. Old Red was the more appropriate nickname for the car after Greg put some miles on it. With a dented fender here and a damaged bumper there, good old Red Rocket had taken quite a beating over time. From the very first day Greg had his learner's permit to his driver's license, he asked Dad if he could take the car out for a spin. Dad gave him permission, but with some clear instructions and restrictions. Greg intended to follow dad's orders. Nevertheless, as soon as he loaded up all his friends in the back seat and blasted the radio, he stretched the boundaries a bit. It wasn't long before he had Dad's car in Ingham's Mills, the nearby town our cousins Sundi and Courtney lived in. Ingham's Mills was even more rural than our own small village. So it was easier to get away with racing down a back road in that neck of the woods. Of course, the guardrail got in the way a bit when they couldn't quite make the ninety-degree corner in time. That's how he lived his life though, on the edge. He was quiet, peaceful, and introverted, unless he was mad. He was loving, compassionate, and protective toward his family, animals, and the underdog. He especially loved animals.

One day when he and Dad were working on a demolition job together at Stoner Lake, they tore out the insulation and found a nest of mice. Greg, of course, wanted to bring them home and adopt them. He and Dad were successfully able to save one out of five mice. What may have seemed like an insignificant rodent to some was life with value to Greg. Although he usually resolved emotions physically in some way when he was mad, he also had a very tender side toward his family, his friends, and Julie. He could beat the living tar out of guys like Jimmer Watson at night, but he also assisted Mom by day when she injured her arm on a machine at Rawlings where she worked. She wasn't able to carry laundry from the basement of the upstairs apartment due to her arm injury so Greg would go out of his way to help our mother carry baskets of laundry up and down the cellar steps to the washer and dryer. It brought him great joy to do so. He loved Mom deeply, and it gave him a sense of satisfaction to care for her tenderly. His relationship with Mom had been broken for some time. Greg never dealt with the unresolved feelings he felt surrounding our parents' divorce and all that had led up to it. Greg had such a deep sense of loyalty to Dad that it skewed his perspective a bit, leaving his relationship with the mother he loved so deeply severed. That changed over time.

I guilted myself about the argument I had with Greg that night when things spiraled so quickly out of control at Dad's house. He was just doing what he normally did. He was coming home with Julie and some friends after a night of partying. It was late, they were loud, and someone was vomiting in the bathroom, which woke my one-year-old-son Zachary. Like a protective mama bear over her cub, I was angry when I came out of my bedroom to scold my brother and his friends for their behavior. I later regretted that when Dad rose from his slumber to see what all the commotion was about. Somehow things escalated and led to a physical confrontation between him and Greg. As a result, Greg packed his belongings, moved out of the home he lived in for many years, and relocated to Mom's apartment in town. I felt responsible and blamed myself for a long time after that, especially considering events that were soon to come. However, as the years passed, my perspective changed a bit, and I could see the good in a bad situation that I regretted. It's often more natural to look at a glass half empty than half full. However, when I am intentional about taking control over my own self-defeating thoughts, I can focus on the positive in a negative situation. I was eventually able to forgive myself—although some days I still beat myself up over fighting with the brother I loved so much—and be grateful that what the devil meant for harm, God used for good. God used that broken place in Greg's relationship with me and Dad to mend Greg's relationship with Mom. For that, I am grateful.

Greg was respectful to those who respected him, and he was well-liked by those he had such relationships with. He was extremely close with his football coach and other assistant coaches. He was also well-liked by his art and band teachers, and he was mutually fond of them. He was equally close to a coach from an opposing team. The football coach of the Clinton team, Mr. Connelly, took specific interest in my brother Greg. He would come to watch Greg play at various games and was intrigued by him. He said that he had more heart than any kid playing high school football he ever saw. After some time, Greg and Mr. Connelly became friends both on and off the football field. Greg respected and looked up to him. Mr. Connelly eventually became the football coach at Greg's alma mater a year or two later. But that was further down the road. In the present moment, as much as Greg was quiet, calm, cool, and collected, he also loved to frolic and have a good time. He was very much a risk-taker his entire life. Even as a young child, he had a mischievous side and often was referred to as a *daredevil.*

Conversely, I could not have been more opposite. What kept me from going down the wayward path of drugs and alcohol was fear. So many of my friends, acquaintances, and even my boyfriend at the time experimented with those types of substances. I very much battled apprehension and anxiety. As a nervous Nellie and worrywart, I was afraid of almost everything that had any potential to harm me or someone I cared about. Unlike me though, Greg wasn't afraid of many things after he overcame his anxiety about the dark. He certainly wasn't transparent about any specific fears. He wasn't afraid to take risks and try new things. To some extent, that was helpful to him, as it is anyone. However, it also very much contributed to his demise.

His demise—yes, I suppose that is where we're at. Quite honestly, I struggle to share much of this part of his story with you. I feel as though I am betraying him in some way. However, if the purpose of this book is help others, then we have no choice but to go down this dark and dreary road—and a dark and dreary road it was indeed. As I ponder, I don't exactly know how it is that Brother ended up off track—well, technically, he was *on* the track. We'll get there soon enough. But for now, he had reached a crossroad in life. I can't identity the exact turning point for when he entered a darker place. I would describe his journey as more of a slow fade. There wasn't a single defining moment where he lost his way. It was a gradual decline. At one time, such a happy-go-lucky and free-spirited child was fading into a pit of depression, despair, and darkness. I'm sure that the crumbling of our family and home life had a lasting impact on him. In fact, I know it did. He was hurting by it all, confused, feeling abandoned, and torn between two parents, siblings, and households. He didn't like turmoil. It affected him. Much in the same way that others end up on a similar path, normal teenage curiosity, experimenting, and learning to spread his own wings and soar from childhood into adolescence factored in as well. Perhaps it also had a little bit to do with trying to fit in and belong. Some of his close friends were on similar paths and dealing with their own struggles. It just made sense that they connected on that level. In the small town we lived in, there wasn't a lot for teenage boys to do socially so they participated in house and back road parties. Most of the time, these types of parties had large amounts of alcohol and drugs. It was easy to become entangled in the web of peer pressure to fit in.

Dad was doing the best he could to raise the boys who lived with him primarily. Since it was just Dad and the two boys living in our old family home, it was understandable that it had become somewhat of a bachelor pad. The nature of their relationships changed as they considered their father more of a friend than authority figure. After all, Dad had become a little more lenient with them than he was with me, partially because the nature of our family dynamics had drastically changed since I was their age, but also because they were boys and Dad had less concerns than he did with me at that same age. There were guidelines and rules. It certainly wasn't a free-for-all. Aware that the boys were dabbling a bit with alcohol, Dad figured that if he banned it entirely, they would rebel even more since it seemed to be what boys their age did. So Dad's philosophy was that he would rather the boys and their friends be safe while being more open about what they were doing rather than placing themselves in harm's way in attempting to keep things secretive. Dad's one non-negotiable rule was no drinking and driving. He always told us kids that if we were ever in a position when the only ride we had home was with a friend who had been drinking, we were to call him at any hour and no questions would be asked. So long as he knew everyone was safe at his house and he confiscated each attendee's key upon arrival, he would occasionally allow the boys to have parties at the house. It wasn't all that uncommon of a concept in the early nineties. It seemed that many of our friends' parents had similar parenting styles at that time.

Of course, there was that one night when my brothers took matters a little too far. They asked Dad if they could have "a few friends" over for "a few beers." He agreed under the usual rules and conditions. He trusted them, probably a little more so than he should have. After all, they hadn't given him much of a reason not to. So Dad went on to his new girlfriend's apartment and allowed the boys to have their little get-together, at least until Grandma Foster drove by. Grandma had a sneaky way of doing just that. Somehow she always seemed to manage to have an informant who would give her all the evidence she needed to show up at parties her grandchildren were at. Years down the road, we learned that her "informants" were our cousins, Mandy and Kay, whom Grandma lived with at that time. It always made for an added element of excitement when Grandma showed up at various parties to grab her grandsons by their ears among their peers and drag them to her little Dodge Neon. There was yet another special occasion in which Grandma would show up uninvited. This house party would require a telephone call to the homeowner, my dad (Grandma's son). She couldn't inform him much over the phone with the loud partygoers and volume on the boom box almost visibly shaking the little ranch house. But she did make her point clear that he needed to get home right away. So Dad left his girlfriend's apartment and drove the half hour trip back home. He reached the top of Barto Hill, where travelers could see mountains and picturesque landscape of the countryside for miles. The canvas would be different that night when Dad reached the top of that hill. From where he was, still a solid 15-minute drive away, it appeared that off in the distance there was a fire, as the entire night sky was illuminated with the glow of flames and clouds of black smoke. When he finally reached his road, he couldn't park in his own driveway which was filled with rows of vehicles that lined the old country back road. He parked as close as he could and made his way to his overpopulated dwelling. As he neared his front yard, he became aware of what it was exactly that was creating the parade of smoke and lights in the sky from a distance. It was a massive bonfire complete with the dog house sitting atop the crackling flames, subtly hidden in the fog of smoke. He headed to the front door on a mission to find his sons who were responsible for this travesty and wring their necks. He was approached by a stranger standing near his front door. "Who are you?"

"I live here! Who are *you*?" Dad responded angrily.

Greg and Jimmy gave him a million and one excuses as to how having a few people over had become a scene out of the movie *Sixteen Candles*. There was a mass exodus of sorts at that point as Greg and Jimmy were in quite a bit of trouble. Part of their punishment was to clean up the mess, ashes from the bonfire included. They were also given a directive that they were responsible for replacing the doghouse they used as firewood.

Wild parties were just a scratch of a shallow surface to a much deeper pit. Smoking cigarettes and drinking alcohol became smoking marijuana. When that combination of cocktails wasn't quite enough to satisfy the curiosity or numb the pain, they also experimented with hard-core drugs. As thoughts invaded their young minds, choices were made in desperate efforts to resolve inner torment. A hit of acid under their tongues, narcotic pills washed down with liquor, crack smoked through a pipe, or a line of cocaine cut with a sharp, double-edged razor and snorted up their noses—they tried just about everything. The strange thing about the pangs of sin and addiction is that it's never satisfied. It always craves more. They could not stop as the circle of life gradually spun on its axis further and further into dimness.

Darker yet was Greg's interest in the underworld, a sixth sense, so to speak. Grandpa Daley had warned us kids about witchcraft and sorcery. He told us that God didn't approve of such activity and that the Bible spoke against it. That's likely the precise reason my mom hated the Ouija board Greg had become so keen of. I'm not even exactly sure where or who he got it from, but he loved that odd plank of black magic. Brother had always been intrigued by the mysteries of wizardry. Even as a child, he loved magic and equally loved performing magic tricks for visitors at our home. He also loved to juggle and taught himself in his early adolescent years. He received a Magic 8-Ball as a child and enjoyed asking the peculiar black sphere filled with liquid questions about the future. Eager for a response, he would give the magical globe a firm shake and await predictions of things to come. Much in the same way, he was intrigued by the large triangular cursor that seemingly shifted across the Ouija board on its own, mysteriously pointing to answers for interrogations about the future. He also had a little doll on the top of his bedpost that he referred to as a voodoo doll of his beloved Julie. When he was mad at Julie about something, he would place a clear plastic cap of an old hairspray can on top of the doll's head. I'm not exactly sure why he did so. Perhaps it represented a dunce cap. When they made up and he wasn't mad at her anymore, he removed the hat from her replica. That's just who he was, a comedian at heart.

Looking back and knowing what I know now that I'm a little older and have some life experiences under my belt, I've grown to view a simplistic, seemingly meaningless game on a board or plastic cap on a doll in a different vein. With some deeper understanding of God's Word hidden in my heart, I've come to understand the deeper waters of witchcraft. Sorcery, the use of spells, divination, or speaking to spirits is clearly condemned in the Bible. The word sorcery in Scripture is always used in reference to an evil or deceptive practice. The Apostle Paul lists sorcery as one of many sinful practices that mark the lives of unbelievers. "Now the works of the flesh are evident: sexual immorality, idolatry, impurity, sensuality, sorcery, enmity, strife ... and things like these. I warn you, as I warned you before, that those who do such things will not inherit the kingdom of God" (Gal. 5:19–21, ESV).

Unfortunately, I believe my brother just didn't know the power and seriousness of what seemed to be a meaningless game of thrones at the time. I don't know if it was in fact the conjuring and trickery of the dark unknown that gave Greg the inherent, preconceived notion that he would die at a young age, but he talked about death on occasion. He had a sense that he would die young. Our family never really understood why he suspected that, but we thought that the Ouija board he had an attachment to gave him that answer on one occasion. He told us that it was revealed to him that he would die at nineteen years old. Of course, verbalizing that sort of thing enraged and caused considerable concern for our parents, and rightly so. He chalked it up to nothing meaningful and just something stupid a game in an imaginary world pointed to. Yet on a deeper level, he seemed to believe it. He talked to Dad a little bit about death and the details of what each of them wanted as their last wishes. They discussed that they both wanted to be buried in their number 25 football jerseys as well as other various details. They confidentially agreed between themselves to honor one another's requests if the inevitable reality of death did come. That's really about all this type of conversation amounted to, an acknowledgment of what will inevitably come to all of us, the day we secretly hope will only occur sometime in the very, very distant future.

12

The Track

You make known to me the path of life; you will fill me with joy
in your presence, with eternal pleasures at your right hand.
—Psalm 16:11 (NIV)

W ell, it's been quite a journey together so far. We have traveled deep and wide to reach this track that has become so significant that it has earned itself a book title. I suppose we've traveled too far to turn back now. Shall we?

It was just another ordinary weekday in our little hometown in Upstate New York on that brisk spring day that would soon bring the month of April showers to a close in 1994. The sound of chirping baby hatchlings resonated in the air. Meteorologists yet again forecasted that April showers would bring May flowers. Officially, springtime in New England, it was a time when barren trees had begun to bud sprigs of hope of what was to come. The purpose of rain in the season prior to summer solstice in the northeast is to bring growth, rebirth, new beginnings, and new life. Rainy days aren't always pleasant in the moment. They can make our surroundings dark, dreary, and just plain messy. Yet, with every passing shower, there is optimism that beauty and new life is burgeoning all around us. There is one certain in a world of uncertainties that can be anticipated. The sunshine will eventually peak through the clouds of darkness and sometimes even bring a spectacularly colorful rainbow along with it. There wasn't much unusual about the time of year in the place where everyone knew your name. It was springtime, which was a celebratory term in the Adirondack Mountains. Old Man Winter usually overstayed his welcome after beating the area with frigid temperatures, ice, sleet, and snow from the previous October forward. It was understandable that most of the locals in town looked forward to this time of year. The atmosphere visibly changed as the warmth of the sunshine and precipitation from nimbus clouds dissipated the accumulation of snow on the ground. Barren old oak trees that had appeared lifeless now blossomed with buds and sprouts of new life. The delicate sound of tiny sparrows chirping and squeaking could be heard in the still of the morning dew from the direction of the straw nests they busily worked to construct.

Although temperatures were still chilly, it was a welcomed respite to go outside without bundling up in heavy winter coats, snow boots, knitted hats, wool scarves, and waterproof gloves. It was the time of year when children tucked away their winter sleds for the season and brought out their bicycles stored away in the garage during midwinter months. It was the time when parents scurried their youngsters to the soccer fields in cleats and shin guards or to the baseball park with their ball cap and leather glove hand-sewn locally at the Rawlings factory where Mom worked as a supervisor. One of the most exciting elements of the month April in this part of the North Country was that my favorite local burger and ice cream drive-in, Green Acres reopened for the summer months after a winter hiatus. Yes, this was most definitely a welcomed time of year in our neck of the woods. The only aspect about this particular April day in 1994 out of the ordinary was that Dad broke his back a few weeks prior, on a roofing project and was temporarily out of work. He was in considerable amount of pain and received medical care for a very serious injury. Other than that unfortunate event, it was a conventional Thursday on April 28, 1994.

School kids were particularly excited. They were about to have an extended four-day weekend since school was scheduled to be closed the next day due to a superintendent's conference day. By the time they would return to school on the following Monday, it would be May, which was significant because the upcoming graduation commencement ceremony was in June. My brother Greg was very much looking forward to that day. It was his senior year. In merely six short weeks, he was scheduled to graduate from high school. Like many high school seniors, he was unsure about what he wanted to do with the rest of his life. He was also hopeful as he contemplated two excellent options available to him. Option one was enlisting in the military. Following in the footsteps of our father, he had recently spoken with a recruiter and was considering enlistment in the air force. He also had a talk with Dad in detail about joining the roofer's union as an apprentice. After many summers of working alongside Dad, he had taken great interest in the profession.

Greg and Julie were amid a breakup. That wasn't all that uncommon. They were very good at breaking up, seeing other people, and getting back together. Young and lacking developmental maturation enough for effective conflict resolution strategies from a difference of opinion, a breakup would follow and they would eventually reconcile. The method to their madness was not unusual for that of high school sweethearts. They were very much learning as they went along in the dating process. Greg had talked to both Mom and Dad about the future with Julie. He expressed that once he graduated, he wanted to get married and have children with Julie. He was leaning a little more toward joining the roofer's union apprenticeship program than a military career and lifestyle. He loved the region on the map where our family had planted roots and had no profound yearning to leave the place he had called home most of his entire life.

Zachary and I were no longer living in Dad's bachelor pad. I recently moved into my own apartment. It wasn't anything fancy; in fact, it was income-based housing. Nonetheless, it was a quaint and cozy home for me and the little boy who had become the center of my entire universe, and that's all that really mattered. I met Harry about eight months prior. Although life wasn't easy as a single mom who had not yet finished college and worked as a front desk switchboard operator at the local hospital for minimum wage salary, circumstances had begun to look up for me a bit. Although we worked in different departments, Harry's mom also worked at the hospital. Our love story is another narrative for an alternative time. The brief version of our now twenty-four-year history is that Harry's mom played matchmaker and became my mother-in-law a couple of years later.

It was just an ordinary Thursday that morning of April 28, 1994. I dropped Zachary off at day care early that morning and went to work my usual seven-to-three shift at the hospital. I was still on an emotional high from the night prior. Harry and I were discussing the possibility of taking our relationship to the next step and getting an apartment together. Although I knew that it wasn't the proper order that God had designed for my life, I bought into modern-day psychology over faith-based practices. I decided that even though it didn't work out the first time, I tried putting the cart in front of the horse and thought that it was still an innovative idea to cohabitate together before the wedding bells. After all, it was a popular way of life at the time, particularly in the liberal state of New York. It just made sense in my mind to really get to know a potential future spouse by means of living together before making the lifelong commitment to marriage. That is all essentially a long explanation around my actual point, which was that I was on an emotional high from the previous night. Harry and I had gone to look at an apartment together in my hometown, rather than where my current apartment was in his hometown. Thus, I was excited about returning to my old stomping grounds. Adding a cherry to the top of the sundae of anticipation, the apartment we considered renting was right at the end of the street where my mom and her new beau lived with my two brothers in a nearby apartment. Not far down the street in the opposite direction was the blue house on Elm Street I so frequently visited where Aunt Me-Me, Uncle Randy, cousins Mandy and Kayla, and Grandma Foster lived. For practical purposes, it was the perfect location.

On our way to view the apartment, we ran into my brother Greg at the end of the street. Harry, Zachary, and I were in my black Grand Am; he was riding his bike. He lived just a few houses up the street with Mom. He recognized my car and pulled up next to the driver's side window. "Are you coming over to Mom's?" he asked.

"Maybe later," I said. "Right now we're on our way to look at that apartment over there. We're running late. We were supposed to be there five minutes ago. Gotta run."

"Oh, okay. Are you coming over to Mom's after your appointment?" he inquired.

"Yeah, probably. We'll see."

We said our good-byes and told one another we loved each other. No matter how grown-up we were, we were a family that always told one another we loved each other at every parting or even to retire for bed each night. We did that since we were toddlers. It was habit.

Harry, Zachary, and I hustled to the driveway of the apartment across the street, and Greg went in the opposite direction on his bike. You never expect a routine encounter or departure to be your last with anyone you love. Oh, how I wish I had—well, I've already said too much too soon. We viewed the apartment, left, and stopped by Mom's place for a few minutes just a few houses up the street. Greg and Jimmy were both out when we visited mom so we left after a little while. This will be significant later on.

The following day was just a regular school day for my brothers. Julie stayed overnight the night before. Although Mom wasn't aware of it at the time, she didn't mind. Greg was over eighteen, essentially an adult. He had his own entrance to the apartment and could come and go as he pleased. It wasn't unusual for Julie to be there. However, she hadn't been regularly at that time due to their breakup. Somehow the two of them were making their way back to one another, although Greg hadn't removed the plastic hairspray "dunce" cap from his Julie doll on his bedpost just yet.

Mom called the boys from work that Thursday morning at seven o'clock as she always did. Greg always answered the phone as it was closest to his bed. This particular morning, Jimmy answered instead. Mom asked, "Where's Greggie?"

"Oh, he's already in the shower," Jimmy replied.

Mom said, "Oh, okay. I was just calling to make sure you were both up and getting ready for school."

He assured her that both he and Greg were up and getting ready to leave for school soon. Greg got out of the shower and was getting dressed. Julie went back to her house to get ready for school. They parted ways as Greg started walking up the school hill. On the way, he met up with Aunt Kim's daughters, Mandy and Kay. When they reached the school building, Greg bid his cousins good-bye and told them that he loved them. It was a day like any other school day. Nothing was out of the ordinary. Greg planned to hang out with friends and classmates later for a night of drinking and partying to kick off their three-day weekend. Greg decided to leave early after lunch. Back in 1994, students could go down street for lunch. We had to have signed permission slips by our parents or guardians at the beginning of each school year to leave the school property during our designated lunch period to go to town. We all typically went to the Food Basket; a local market for grocery and convenience items. There was also a deli at the back of the store where subs and other lunch items were sold. We usually only had time enough to eat the food en route back to school. Nevertheless, it was a pleasant freedom we looked forward to. It was an opportunity to socialize with friends and get outside in the sunshine and fresh air for half an hour or so. It wasn't uncommon for my brothers to not go back to school after lunch and even skip classes altogether on any given day, not that there wouldn't be consequences to such poor choices. It's just that consequences were somewhat unimportant to them. They in a sense marched to the beat of their own drums.

Greg wrote Julie a note that said, "I left early" inside of her locker door and exited the school for the last time. Jimmy left at some point early as well as some other friends. They spent the rest of the afternoon hanging out and making plans for parties later in the evening. Greg returned to Mom's apartment, which was across the street from a well-known shoemaking factory. One of Greg's good friends from the fantastic five worked there. Richie worked on the third floor directly next to the window facing Mom's apartment. Richie heard some yelling. It was common for Greg to call out to Richie from his bedroom window across the street. "Hey, Miller! Let's hit the tracks tonight!" Greg hollered.

"I'll talk to you later after I get out!"

Greg went to Richie's house after his shift. They talked for a bit. Greg tried to talk Richie into meeting up with him and some others later in the evening at the tracks where there was going to be a party. Richie couldn't go. He had to go back to work later that night to help his girlfriend Melissa's father out at the shoe factory. They shook hands and made plans to see each other the following day. Greg appeared to be in a pleasant mood to others he crossed paths with throughout that day. However, at some point, his temperament shifted. He became troubled by something. He visited his friend Jim on and off throughout that afternoon and early evening. He brought a bottle of whiskey with him when he arrived at Jim's apartment and had begun drinking. Sometimes when he drank, his frame of mind automatically changed depending on the type of alcohol or amount he was consuming. So it's hard to say with certainty if this was just one of those instances or if something had indeed happened to upset him. He did admit to Jim that he was troubled by the fact that Julie started seeing his long-term arch rival he had bad blood with.

There was a lot going on in Greg's mind and heart. He didn't really let others who didn't intimately know him into the broken places of his soul. Even those who were closest to him, he only let in to a certain extent. He was dealing with the heartbreak of a breakup. He had recently been in trouble with the law for a fight he had been implicated in and was facing an assault charge for his involvement. He was extremely worried about the impact that would have on his future. With graduation day right around the corner, the pressure to figure out the impending future loomed heavily over his head. Already battling discouragement and depression, he did what he and so many others often do when struggling emotionally. He drowned himself in alcohol and drugs to numb the pain. The more his thoughts raged war, the more he consumed to numb the pain. The more intoxicated and high he became, the deeper his intense emotions drove him further into despair. It was a vicious cycle, one that spun completely out of control. He often expressed his emotions associated with hurt and brokenness through anger. Intense feelings of fury fueled a mind-set toward aggression and desire to release the pain he felt through combat. He reached a point in his mental state where he was looking for warfare. Jim encouraged him to stay a while and cool off. Greg heeded the advice. They had more alcohol and other substances together. Greg's other best friend Gerald was also there at Jim's apartment that day. Greg and Gerald had been squabbling about something. They did that often. They fought like brothers and then helped each other up and went to have a beer together after. That's sort of what it was like that day. They just acted as if nothing happened and had some drinks together and talked. Greg finally left around dusk that evening. He eventually ended up at Boyer Pit, which was deep into the country. It was one of their preferred places to party. Off the beaten path and deep in the woods, it was a desirable location with as much privacy as the crowds that gathered there, needed away from adults, parents, or police. Rumor had it that there was a huge party that night, which had already begun earlier that afternoon.

The details between where we are now and where we are headed are fuzzy. For outsiders like me, my parents, extended family members, and the entire community who were not physically there with him that night, it's difficult to imagine what may have been when so many pieces to a large puzzle are missing. Like a camera lens that goes in and out of focus, much about a night that was the absolute most horrific day of our lives, has become blurred in the transition between the past and present. So much trauma, so much pain. I imagine much of the amnesia of events is subconsciously intentional. Sometimes it's the only way to really keep going in life when the agony of a traumatic event keeps us locked in the prison of selective memory lapse. Maybe it's God's gift to those left behind to eventually forget the details of a life event that is so incredibly unbearable to reflect upon. For others still who were in the midst, perhaps they were as inebriated as my brother that night. They had been drinking and partaking in an assortment of illicit drugs for hours. It was a celebratory point in time with no school the following day, a full three-day weekend, it was finally spring after a long winter, and graduation was right around the bend.

Greg's demeanor was not like the others. By the time he arrived at the party, he was completely wasted. Not in his right state of mind and grappling with intense emotions and anger, he was belligerent and prone to instigating conflict. Our youngest brother Jimmy, usually right at Greg's side, was already at the party since early in the day. The crowd at Boyer Pit was primarily made up of Greg's friends and peers, even some cousins. They didn't want a confrontation with him. They cared about him and knew he had had way too much to drink. For strangers in the midst, it was more a principle of semantics. Anyone with any common sense whatsoever, even masked with drugs and alcohol, knew better than to go into battle with Greg Foster. After all, he had a reputation. It was more likely than not that any opponent on the other end risked serious injuries if they crossed him. Other than factors of common sense and sentimentality, they were there simply to have a good time and wanted to enjoy their night. So after Greg tried to take several different partygoers' beers out of their hands, the consensus at the party was that it was time for him to leave. Some of his closest friends spewed statements such as, "Why don't you leave? Just go! You're nothing but trying to cause trouble right now! Just get out of here! Nobody wants you here!" If only they had known that those would be the last words they would ever speak to their best friend, classmate, teammate, cousin, and brother. But they didn't know. We take so much for granted in this world. We live assuming tomorrow will come. Yet the reality is, tomorrow isn't promised. Not many of us live our lives as if we are engaging with someone we love and care about for the very last time.

Greg did exactly what was asked of him. He took his hurt, anger, rejection, and intoxication and left. He was in pursuit of a girl from his school who was a senior and graduating soon. He was unsure of his future with Julie at that point since she had also somewhat moved on and had little concern for the future or consequence. Only focused on his present pain and circumstances, he left the party with a friend who was the key to this girl's presence. This guy had been a long-time friend of Greg's. They had known each other since they were just children and he could often be found near a beautiful cheerleader Greg was pursuing that night. It was a disturbing scene as they left the party and tore out of the sandpit like mad men. His friend's Volkswagen Rabbit tires kicked up dirt as they spun "doughnuts" in the midst of the crowd. Out the window of the passenger seat, Greg was yelling profanities at the crowd. The girl Greg was interested in and her friend followed behind them separately in another vehicle. The plan was to head down to the tracks to continue the evening shenanigans. It was the place Greg recently told Dad about where he and his friends hung out. Right at the bridge that crosses over the East Canada Creek, separating two counties, there was a private entrance to an access road to some farm land out in the countryside just west of the Montgomery County line. The dirt-and-gravel road cut through a wooded area and ran parallel with the brook. At the end of the access road, about one-tenth of a mile south of route 5, was an area cleared of trees and brush right next to a train track. The area was used for train track construction equipment. I'm not sure how they found the location, but it was a site that they had just recently begun going to.

In fact, Greg had just told dad about the new party location the night before. He told Dad that he and some friends had been going to the train tracks to hang out and have parties, which was alarming to our father. What was even more astonishing was the report that he gave dad that he and his friends would stand on top of the bridge that went over the tracks while CSX freight trains went through beneath them. It was a stunt they performed to see who could hold on the longest. Greg said that it gave them a rush as the train went through, which violently shook and rattled the boys sitting atop the bridge holding on to the iron and steel for their lives. Dad was shocked and enraged about the dangerous activity Greg and his friends had been experimenting with. Dad gave him orders not to ever go there or do that again. Greg assured Dad that he wouldn't.

To back up a little to events leading up to this point, Greg stopped by Aunt Kim's house and ate leftovers and brownies for dinner on Wednesday evening, as he often did so. Dad was there also for coffee and to visit his sister, mother, brother-in-law, and nieces. Greg asked Dad if they could go out on the front porch to talk privately. It was during that conversation that Greg asked if he could move back home. Eleven months earlier, Greg had an argument with me that escalated out of control and he moved into Mom's apartment where he had been living for nearly a year. It wasn't that he didn't enjoy living with Mom. He loved her deeply and was glad to have worked through some things that were causing distance between them during that time. It would soon come to mean more than they even realized at the time. It was just that he longed for his home. He wanted to return to his basement bedroom where he had his drum set, the camp he built in the woods behind the house, and all that he loved about being there. It was his and Dad's bachelor pad, and he missed it. Dad and Greg apologized to one another prior to that night and were on peaceful terms, however, they desired to go back to the way things were.

The plan was that he would begin moving some things home on that three-day weekend off from school. Arrangements and conditions for returning home had been agreed upon, and a promise had been made to honor dad's request to never go to the track again. Yet, just twenty-four hours later in an altered state of mind, a choice had been made and a promise broken. He and a buddy were doing exactly what he promised Dad he wouldn't do again. They were trying to meet up with two girls at the track. When the girls arrived, Greg and his buddy were already there. Music was playing, and they were set up to party there for a while. Others were supposed to be joining them later in the night. It was just dusk.

Greg was a daredevil, a risk-taker. He lived life on the edge. There was one more reason than mere adrenaline rush to disobey Dad's orders that Thursday night. There were two girls down there, one of whom Greg was trying to impress with death-defying antics. So the two boys climbed the steel trusses to the top of the old rusty bridge and awaited a freight train to round the bend. They could see the train's bright headlights as they approached from a mile away. It was much easier to hear an oncoming freight train than a passenger train, although not nearly as loud as one would expect. Unlike the fast, smooth, and sleek passenger train, the cargo train rumbles as it gets closer. The anticipation as the sound of thunder drew closer was the appetizer for what was to come. The whistle sounding like a forlorn call in the night was equally part of the rush. It was the moment they waited for, the violent shaking and trembling of their bodies against the steel as they clung to the bridge. The force of the train almost took their breath away when the locomotive passed beneath them. They successfully managed to maintain their grip around the steel as the cargo train passed through beneath them. The strange thing about adrenaline rush is that it is never fully satisfied. It always craves more. Having overcome a death-defying stunt on multiple occasions, they wanted to take the fear factor and risk level to new heights.

I'm not sure what goes through a teenage boy's mind when deciding to play chicken with a train. Didn't they understand the level of danger? I suppose that was precisely the effect they were going for. I'm not even sure whose idea it was. My family has never really received many answers to all the questions we have. So many pieces of a very complicated puzzle were never filled in. Other blanks and missing fragments are filled with discrepancies. Sometimes a family has no choice but to accept what is and move forward through gaps, given tragic circumstances. The two boys stood on the brown-colored steel track. The train signal lights lit red on the eastbound track and green on the westbound track. Like driving on the highways in Europe, the train track is set up just the opposite of how we travel on United States roadways. The red light in the eastbound lane indicated that no train should be coming from that direction. The green light on the westbound side indicated that a train was en route. It only takes a matter of seconds when a sleek silver bullet is moving at high speed down the slats of the track, which bounce up and down as the train passes through. Unlike the first one, it wasn't a freight train approaching this time. It was a commuter train. Far more expeditiously, Amtrak train number 289 hurtled down the railroad ties at a speed of 103 mph. Those are the facts we know. Beyond that is a mystery of conflicting reports and accounts. One account is the two teenage boys stood on the track. Greg stood on the left and his friend stood to his right.

They waited. Their heartbeats raced as adrenaline rushed to their heads. The oncoming headlights were almost blinding as the locomotive neared. Unlike large steam engines which thundered along the rails, modern railcars glide with low friction. As the crushed rock underneath the tracks helps diminish the noise that usually serves as a warning, there was utter silence until the silver bullet was upon them. The piercing light and unexpected silence created a misconception of distance. Alcohol and likely other substances that very much delay response times, coupled with other effected factors such as balance and coordination, were likely the ideal recipe for an accident of great magnitudes. All ingredients necessary for a tragic outcome were present, as was the foolishness, impulsivity, and lack of judgment for the teenage boys. In an instant, a not-well-thought-out choice created a lifetime of pain, regret, and trauma for all involved.

From inside the train, the conductor was positioned near the engineer. There had been a report from the freight train engineer who passed through the area earlier that there were people near the track in the vicinity and two boys were on top of the train bridge as it traveled through. The black box recorder chronicled the communication between the engineer and conductor of Amtrak train number 289. "There are two boys on the track!" They sounded the horn on the train but the boys weren't moving. They sounded again. Approaching at lightning speed, there was no time to put on the brakes. Unlike driving a vehicle, a sudden application of the emergency brakes on a train at that speed could potentially derail entire cars full of passengers en route to Niagara Falls, New York. The train engineer stared into the eyes of two boys standing in front of his train as it hurtled toward them at more than 100 mph. The boys looked back at the driver through squinted eyes. "Come on! Get off the track! Get off the track!" the engineer pleaded with the boys within the earshot of only himself and the conductor.

13

Sudden Impact

*As he neared Damascus on his journey, suddenly
a light from heaven flashed around him.*

—Acts 9:3 (NIV)

The world was black, silent, cold, and lifeless for a split second. As if in slow motion, time stood still. "Oh my God! We hit him! We hit him!" The engineer and conductor immediately went into crisis response mode. In all their years of training, nothing could have prepared them for this gruesome moment as they found themselves trapped within what seemed to be a scene from a horror film.

Shockingly, the sound of his body hitting the front end of the train headfirst, the jolt they felt upon impact, and the sight of the blood-covered windshield played over and over in their minds. With high speeds of over 100 mph, the engineer applied the emergency brake. The brakes hissed and screeched and the couplings clanked as the silver bullet gradually slowed down to a stop a mile down the track. Unlike a motor vehicle, there's no evasive action that can be taken with a train. Swerving or slamming on the brakes isn't an option. The average Amtrak passenger car weighs about sixty-five tons. An Amtrak train with one locomotive and six cars weighs about 540 tons or 1.08 million pounds. That only accounts for the train itself and does not account for the passengers.

Once the train had finally come to a stop and all passengers were safe, crisis response efforts began. The engineer called in the incident to Amtrak headquarters who notified police and emergency personnel. The conductor fled the train and ran back one mile to where the accident occurred. Once the engineer called the appropriate chain of command and secured the train, he ran a mile back to where the impact had occurred just behind the conductor. The scene was horrific. Together they found my brother's body, which had been thrown seventy-five feet from the track where impact had occurred, mangled and alone. The three teenagers with him at the time of the incident were no longer there. It wasn't long before the landscape surrounding the train track was swarmed with emergency vehicles, state police, local police, the county coroner, ambulances, the fire department, and news media.

The engineer and conductor were completely distraught. They were the last two people to see my brother before his tragic fate. A scene such as this one is traumatizing. As the engineer fixed his eyes on the carnage, he thought as he analyzed every detail, *Did I put the brakes on soon enough? Did I react fast enough?*

Back at home, the environment had become equally disconcerting. Dad had an intense conversation on the phone with his ex-girlfriend for quite a while. By this time, my dad had a child with his girlfriend (who he was no longer with at the time) so Greg, Jimmy, and I had a two-year-old half brother named Jacob. We called him Jake for short. Due to the large age gap, our relationship with him resembled more that of an aunt or uncle and nephew than a sibling. Either way, it didn't matter. We accepted and loved him. He lived with his mom full time so he wasn't always with us. However, whenever Dad had weekly scheduled visitation with him, Greg, Jimmy, and I tried to spend time with him as often as we could. So Dad had been on the phone with Jake's mom that evening. He had the television on in the background but only half paying attention to it as he was preoccupied. A breaking news report come across the screen. The local WKTV news station reporter was on the location of an accident involving an Amtrak train. The report was live and captured a disturbing image on camera. There was a body lying near the tracks covered by a white sheet. However, the exposed sneakers on the feet of the covered body were recognizable to Dad. They were just like that of my brother Greg. He had just received them, and to our knowledge, this particular type of sneakers was new to the market. Thus far, Greg was one of the only teens in our cozy hometown who owned a pair.

There was a story behind those sneakers. Greg desperately needed a new pair as his were old and tattered. He asked Mom for a new pair of sneakers. He coveted a pair just like Rocky Balboa's. They were black canvas Adidas running shoes with three white stripes down the side. These Adidas sneakers cost about a hundred dollars in 1994. For a struggling single mother of three and employed by a baseball factory at that time when wages were not what they are today, that amount for a pair of sneakers for just one child was just not something Mom could afford. So Greg did what many teenage boys from a split family would do. He strategically played Mom and Dad like a fiddle. I can't say I wasn't guilty of similar tactics, nor was Jimmy. After all, if we had to have our lives in upheaval and redefine ourselves as coming from a broken home, we were going to be sure to make it worth our while. So he went to Dad with a similar request. Not long after Greg pleaded his case, Dad went out and purchased him a new pair of sneakers just like what he had described, only in white.

In the meantime, Mom couldn't get the sneakers off her mind. She knew that her son really needed new shoes. His current pair was so worn. He really had his heart fixed on the Rocky Balboa replicas. Under the circumstances, she hadn't had an opportunity to do much for him in recent years as their relationship became strained. He had been working hard and recently achieved honor roll status in school, no easy feat for him. He struggled academically as he was dyslexic. Likely, in our day and age, he may have even been diagnosed with ADHD. However, such disorder wasn't commonly diagnosed back then as it is today. Mom applied for a credit card, and to her astonishment, she was approved. She didn't have a great deal of prior experience with having her very own credit card. Credit cards weren't as popular back then, and debit cards were nonexistent. We paid for most every purchase in cash or by check. She was so excited to go out and purchase those sneakers for Greg. She presented them to him on his birthday in February just a couple of months prior. He was equally as excited to receive them as she was to give them. I don't think he ever told Dad the difference or Mom. He didn't want to hurt either of their feelings. After all, not only did he have new sneakers, but he had two pairs that he really had his heart set on in two different colors. Mom paid the shoes off little by little each month when her credit card bill came. Even after, well... Dad recalled his conversation with Greg the night before when Greg informed Dad where he and his friends had been going and what they had been doing. Dad became nauseated. He knew he had to leave as soon as possible. He had to find his son and ensure that he was safe. He was in an intense phone conversation with his ex-girlfriend and repeatedly told her that he needed to hang up and find Greg.

In the meantime, a state police officer was trying to call Dad but getting a busy signal. In 1994, call waiting and caller ID did not exist. If a phone was in use, the other party calling would get a busy signal. When he could not get through, the officer eventually had the operator interrupt the line for an emergency. The trooper conveyed information to dad that any good parent would be terrified to ever receive. He told Dad that there had been an accident and that his son had been hit by a train. Barely able to respond as the news literally took his breath away, Dad asked about Greg's condition through the lump in the pit of his throat. He grabbed hold of the wall nearby. He was already suffering with mobility due to injuring his back a couple of weeks earlier. His knees became weak and he felt as if the weight of his own stature was forcing him to the floor. The trooper said that Greg was okay but had a fractured leg and other various injuries then instructed Dad to report to the local hospital where he was being transported to. Dad frantically called Mom but her line was busy as well. He then called his sister, Aunt Kim, where his mother lived, to notify them of what had happened and directed them to meet him at the hospital. Grandma Foster was told to contact my brother Jimmy and me. That's when I got "the call."

"There's been an accident. Your brother Greg was hit by a train. He has a broken leg and some other injuries. Your father told me to tell you to go to the hospital. He will meet you there," said Grandma Foster, out of breath and upset on the other end of the phone.

Unable to reach my mother on the phone, Dad drove to her apartment on his way to the hospital. He banged on her front door, but she didn't answer. She was already in bed for the night. He had no choice but to open the front door entrance to the apartment building and hollered upstairs, "There's been an accident involving Greggie! We need to get to the hospital!" He quickly returned to his car to go to the hospital. En route, Dad spotted dozens of emergency vehicles with flashing lights in the distance in the same direction of the track where he knew Greg had been frequenting. As he arrived at the fork in the road where he needed to turn right to go to the hospital or left toward the track, he made a split decision to make a detour to the scene. He parked his vehicle at the end of the access road off the main highway that led to the track. He couldn't drive any further. The road was lined with emergency vehicles. He ran on foot the rest of the way up the long dirt-and-gravel road through the wooded area alongside the East Canada Creek to the train track. When he got there, he saw a sheet-covered body on the ground. He attempted to run toward the body but was stopped by the state police on the scene. Completely frantic, he screamed and pleaded with them, "That's my son! That's my son!" Dad was out of his mind with panic and utter hysteria.

The police were holding him back as he attempted to get to his son. They threw him to the ground and handcuffed him to stop him. "This is a crime scene! You cannot go over there! Go to the hospital! He is being brought there now!"

Knowing that his choices at that point were to leave and go to the hospital or be arrested for interfering with a crime scene investigation, Dad agreed to leave. The police released Dad, removing the handcuffs from wrists. He ran back to his vehicle and hastily drove to the hospital. Upon arrival, the scene was horrifying. Mom, her boyfriend, and some of her family was there. Dad's sister and one of his brothers were also present. My brother Jimmy arrived with a large group of his and Greg's friends. They waited and waited for seemingly an incredibly long time for some answers. All that any of us had received up to that point was extremely vague information.

Harry and I were heading to the hospital from my apartment after I had received the call. With limited facts and in a state of confusion, we knew little of the details or where the accident had occurred. As we neared the bridge over the East Canada Creek on the way to the hospital, we saw masses of flashing red lights and emergency vehicles in the distance off the main road. We had no knowledge of where the accident was so I didn't suspect that what we were witnessing was related to the accident involving my brother. After all, my apartment was not in the same town I grew up in. My brothers didn't hang out in that direction, at least to my knowledge. I assumed that the accident involving my brother happened closer to home. As we made our way across the bridge, an ambulance pulled out of an access road just ahead of us. We followed it all the way down route 5 to the hospital. The ambulance traveled along just ahead of us. We followed it all the way to the hospital. When we reached the hospital, the ambulance turned in the direction of the emergency department entrance. However, it proceeded around to the back of the hospital. I worked at the hospital and knew that the morgue was in that direction. I didn't know who, if anyone was in the back of the ambulance.

Harry and I parked in the parking lot in front of the hospital and proceeded to walk up the hill to the side of the hospital where the emergency department entrance was. As we turned the corner, the view ahead was troubling. There were multitudes of people. It was chaos. People were weeping, wailing, screaming, embracing one another, and collapsing to the ground. It was as if time stood still and I was looking through the lens of a camera that was not entirely in focus. The events around me seemed to be playing out in slow motion. As I stepped closer, I began to recognize many of the faces of the people gathered, distraught in appearance. *Why are they all here?* My dad was there and seemed distressed. Aunt Kim and Uncle George were next to him. I was told that my dad would meet me at the hospital. *But why are the others here at this hour?* My mind wandered; my thoughts spiraled out of control.

As I ran in the direction of my dad, I saw a woman lying up ahead on the hill in front of the emergency room main entrance. She was screaming a horrifyingly deep, writhing scream. I shudder just recalling it in my mind. I can still almost hear the heartbreaking sound echo in my head. There was a crowd gathered around her. As the people who were assembled around her repositioned themselves,

I caught a glimpse of the woman. "Mom?" I shouted as I sprinted to my mother's side. "Mom, what is going on?"

I couldn't quite make out what she was verbalizing. She just kept repeating over and over again, "He wanted eggs! He wanted me to make him eggs! All he ever wanted was for me to make him eggs!" She wept, screamed, and moaned in agony.

Shortly after the ambulance pulled into the area behind the hospital, Dad and some others waited in the emergency waiting room to get information from the medical personnel. The attending physician entered the waiting room and asked for the parents. Mom was still outside as the family around her attempted to get her off the road to her vehicle or someplace more suitable than the middle of the road. So when Dr. Boyer asked Dad if he would like to get Greg's mother, Dad told him that she was in no condition to speak with him. The doctor took Dad off to the side privately and explained the extent and nature of my brother's injuries. He followed that description with the two most horrific words a parent could ever hear about their child. "He's dead."

The physician was very abrupt and matter-of-fact, almost lacking bedside manner. My dad didn't understand the apathy and lack of compassion in that moment. However, he couldn't focus on that. There were certainly more tragic matters at hand. How was he going to go tell the rest of the family, my mother, or his other children? How was he going to do any of what lied ahead? In fact, how was he even going to survive losing his child? Dr. Boyer told dad that he needed to accompany him to the morgue and make a positive identification on the body. Dad, in a deep state of shock and denial, could not understand or accept what was being asked of him. Almost robotic in demeanor and numb, he followed the doctor like a zombie along the hallway and down several flights of steps that led to the morgue. Aunt Kim and Uncle George followed closely behind. After all, he would need his big brother and only sister for the assignment before him. In confusion and denial, Dad asked Dr. Boyer several times, "Why are we going down here? Why aren't we going into the emergency room?"

Dr. Boyer responded, "Because he's not there. He's in the morgue. He's dead. I've told you, Mr. Foster, he's dead."

It's as if Dad heard the words being spoken to him but was not processing or comprehending what was being said. They finally reached the dungeonlike morgue. Dad, his sister, his brother, and the physician entered the cold, dark, and eerie space. The state police accompanying them stood outside the door in the hallway. Aunt Kim placed her arm around her brother not only to support, love, and console him, but also to physically hold him upright.

The doctor proceeded over to a wall of drawers and pulled out the slide where a body laid covered in a sheet. For a moment, insensitive to a father's heart and almost as if procedurally checking off an item on a document, Dr. Boyer pulled back the sheet and asked in a businesslike manner, "Mr. Foster, is this your son?"

The image was more than Aunt Kim could bear as the body of her beloved nephew she loved so deeply was revealed. Lying there lifeless, cold, and mangled with severe head trauma, Greg was almost unrecognizable but for the tattoo on his arm, which was the only sure way Dad could make a positive identification. Barely able to stand, Dad rested his head on his son's body and embraced him as he wept gut-wrenching sobs. The doctor and Dad's siblings stepped out of the room to allow him some privacy to say good-bye to his son. As my father wept over his lifeless, dismembered son, he overheard two voices outside the door in the hallway. What he heard took him over the edge from grief to anger. "It's just another scumbag off the streets."

Dad darted out the doors of the morgue in fury and found two state troopers standing there who had just made the callous and cruel statement. Dad physically charged and screamed at them, "That was my son! That was my son!"

For the second instance that evening within a couple of hours, the two officers threw my grieving dad to the ground and handcuffed him yet again. His brother ran to him, assuring the officers, "I've got him! I've got him!"

They agreed to release my dad to his brother's custody. Under the circumstances, the police agreed not to arrest him. The county coroner was standing nearby, awaiting the formal legalities such as signing official custody of my brother's body over to his custody to be transported to the funeral home. Uncle George and Aunt Kim nearly carried Dad out of the building outside to the fresh air to face his next challenge, telling my mom that her son was gone and Jimmy and me that our brother was gone.

Dad made his way to the parking lot where we finally got my mom inside of her vehicle. I was standing at her passenger door awaiting answers. As my dad approached the car, Mom asked, "Is he dead?"

"Yes, he's gone," Dad answered with barely a voice left to speak.

Mom started screaming. "No! No! No! It's not true! You're lying! It's not true!" She was out of her mind with grief. Everyone was embracing and weeping. Nothing made sense.

"Grandma told me on the phone that he's okay! They said he only had a broken leg! They said he was okay!" As bewilderment and panic waged war in my mind, the earth beneath my feet seemed to sway so rapidly that I was losing my balance. Dark sorrow and anguish was so cavernous within the depth of my soul that my heart physically throbbed and ached. The pain felt like a double-edged sword slicing and puncturing my flesh in every area that was not otherwise numb. Grief draped itself around me like an invisible yet almost tangible heavy force. The weight of an incredible presence of darkness weighed my shoulders down and forced my entire being forward as I doubled over in despair. Like waves crashing against me in a category four hurricane, it was difficult to see clearly through tears that gushed from my eyes like an ocean.

With my hands pressed firmly against either side of the temples on my head, I caught a glimpse of my little brother. He was a child who was running toward me, smiling and laughing. He seemed so happy. The sun reflected off his straight, strawberry blonde hair that framed the freckles on his face. My eyes struggled to focus. Regardless of how I was turning the lens at the end of a camera to adjust the blurriness, the reality struck hard that he wasn't there anymore but lived only in my memory. Nothing conceivably prepares a family for an incomprehensible moment such as this. Nightmares of this magnitude don't materialize in our own family trees comfortably rooted in our own backyards. Surely God would spare our family of the pangs of death and tragedy. We were *good* people. I mean, we weren't a perfect family. I don't know any perfect family. We had issues but we were good. We had loving hearts, we were kind and giving, and we even attended church occasionally. Tragedies like this happen in other people's families. But they never strike this close to home.

Angry and out of my right mind with grief, I began yelling at the crowd, "What do you mean he's gone? You're lying! Why would you say that? I was just told on the phone that he only had a broken leg!" In shock and denial, I refused to accept their answer.

My father embraced me as I wept inconsolably. "I'm sorry! I'm sorry!" he apologized over and over again. I fell to the ground with my mother in the parking lot next to the open passenger side door. We laid on the cold, hard asphalt in a fetal position together.

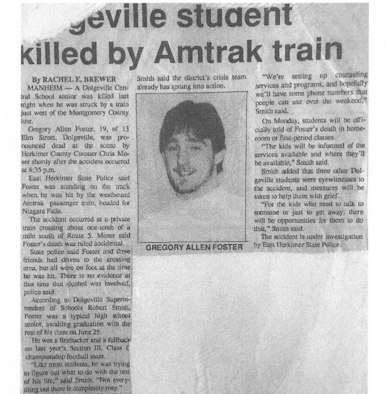

geville student
killed by Amtrak train

By RACHEL E. BREWER

MANHEIM — A Dolgeville Central School senior was killed last night when he was struck by a train just west of the Montgomery County line.

Gregory Allen Foster, 19, of 13 Elm Street, Dolgeville, was pronounced dead at the scene by Herkimer County Coroner Chris Moser shortly after the accident occurred at 8:35 p.m.

East Herkimer State Police said Foster was standing on the track when he was hit by the westbound Amtrak passenger train, headed for Niagara Falls.

The accident occurred at a private train crossing about one-tenth of a mile south of Route 5. Moser said Foster's death was ruled accidental.

State police said Foster and three friends had driven to the crossing area, but all were on foot at the time he was hit. There is no evidence at this time that alcohol was involved, police said.

According to Dolgeville Superintendent of Schools Robert Smith, Foster was a typical high school senior, awaiting graduation with the rest of his class on June 25.

He was a linebacker and a fullback on last year's Section III, Class C championship football team.

"Like most students, he was trying to figure out what to do with the rest of his life," said Smith. "Not everything out there is completely rosy."

Students at Dolgeville High School had the day off today due to a Superintendent's Conference Day, but

Smith said the district's crisis team already has sprung into action.

GREGORY ALLEN FOSTER

"We're setting up counseling services and programs, and hopefully we'll have some phone numbers that people can use over the weekend," Smith said.

On Monday, students will be officially told of Foster's death in homeroom or first-period classes.

"The kids will be informed of the services available and where they'll be available," Smith said.

Smith added that three other Dolgeville students were eyewitnesses to the accident, and measures will be taken to help them with grief.

"For the kids who need to talk to someone or just to get away, there will be opportunities for them to do that," Smith said.

The accident is under investigation by East Herkimer State Police.

14

The Lord Is My Shepherd

Even though I walk through the valley of the shadow
of death, I will fear no evil, for You are with me;
Your rod and Your staff, they comfort me.
—Psalm 23:4 (NASB)

The hours and days ahead were surreal. As life instantly flashed before my eyes, nothing made sense. Traumatized and in a state of shock, I was barely functional. I knew my primary role for such a time as this. I recognized that I needed to take care of my parents, especially my mother. My dad was going through unspeakable grief, in disbelief and very much in a state of denial and confusion. Desiring answers to all the questions our family had, he tried to be strong for the rest of us. Although he was dying a slow death inside the depth of his soul, he presented himself as a rock for the rest of us even though we didn't expect him to be. Mom had absolutely no ability to muster up any form of solidarity. We feared the worst. She simply would not survive a travesty of this magnitude.

With grave concerns for her well-being, family members called Mom's primary care physician and explained the circumstances. Her doctor called in a prescription for a sedative to the local pharmacy. There certainly was no medication that would be an effective anecdote or healing balm to remedy the intense pain she was in, having just lost her son. However, medication for this type of situation would produce some type of calming effect and provide short-term relief of anxiety, panic, and agitation. It also was effective in aiding her to sleep off a large majority of the hours in a twenty-four-hour time period. Mom's beau, her sisters, and I took turns in looking after her 24-7. When I wasn't with Mom, I was with Dad, checking on his well-being, assisting him with funeral arrangements, and writing Greg's obituary and other matters that must be attended to. Equally concerned for my dad's state of mind was my aunt Kim, who stayed at his side nearly every hour. Aunt Kim was dealing with her own intense grief. She and Greg had always been so close. She was also horrifically traumatized going into the morgue with Dad to be a support system for him in his darkest hour. She knew we needed her assistance and provided as much help as we needed in making all the necessary decisions and arrangements that needed to be made.

The entire community was devastated. Tragedy of this magnitude was not something that struck this small hometown frequently. After all, we were that family from that town and that high school now identified as that breaking news story. We were the lead story for days on all the local TV news stations and on the front page displayed on newspaper stands in local businesses in the region. Extended family members attempted to shield us from watching the news or reading newspapers. They even placed a call to the local news stations to stop broadcasting the scene of the train accident and my brother lying on the side of the track covered in a white sheet. We were told to turn the TV off if it was difficult to watch. Crisis intervention efforts went in full effect at the local high school Greg attended, my alma mater. Counseling services and programs were set up and emergency phone numbers were provided for students and staff over the weekend until Monday when school would be back in session and students were officially informed of Greg's death in their first-period classes. Although regularly scheduled classes would resume after a three-day weekend, students and faculty were given an option to take a leave of absence to attend funeral services. In fact, arrangements were made for school buses to be used as transportation for students to attend funeral services.

Dad contacted Coach Walczak who was absolutely devastated to learn about the tragic death of one of his most valued football players and a boy he deeply cared for both on and off the field. Greg told Dad long before this tragedy occurred that if anything ever happened to him, he wanted to be buried in his football jersey. In carrying out his son's wishes, Dad and Coach Walczak mutually decided that number twenty-five would be retired, never to be worn by any future player on the Dolgeville Blue Devils team again. Coach Walczak gave Dad both Greg's home and away jerseys. He was to be buried in his away jersey, and the home jersey was given to the family. Dad brought Greg's treasured jersey to Mr. Moser, the funeral director responsible for preparing my brother for burial and the funeral services. He was given instructions that Greg was to be buried in his football jersey. He also scheduled a meeting to write the obituary, to go over funeral arrangements, and all other official matters that none of us expected to be planning for. After all, we were supposed to be preparing for a graduation party in just six weeks, not a funeral.

No parent ever plans to write their nineteen-year-old child's obituary, pick out a coffin and gravestone, and plan their funeral. Our family was equally unprepared for the daunting task at hand. As grueling as it was, it had to be done. As much as our family was not prepared emotionally to select Greg's casket and write his obituary, we were equally unprepared for the exorbitant expenses. It was an extremely restrictive season in our family financially. Mom and dad were divorced, living separate lives, and trying to make ends meet on single incomes with three dependents to support. They were both blue-collar workers. Mom was employed as a supervisor at the Rawlings factory, and Dad was a roofer in the union. He had a very serious work-related accident several weeks prior and was out of work at the time. Disability pay had not yet become effective. Once it finally did, it was only half of Dad's normal salary, which would not cover the monthly budget, let alone funeral expenses. In 1994, an average funeral in a small town like ours was equivalent to an average cost of about seven thousand dollars. That was certainly not a figure our family could manage to spare at that time. If there's anything positive that can come from a tragedy such as this, it can often pull families together. Dad's brother loaned him the money, which was reimbursed over time. Mom was barely functional, barely surviving. She was not able to handle details such as writing her son's obituary or picking out his casket and gravestone. So Dad, Aunt Kim, and I did our best to attend to those details.

It all happens so quickly when tragedy strikes so close to home. My precious brother I just talked to Wednesday evening was taken from us on Thursday night, and now we were planning his funeral. A viewing for family and friends to pay their respects was scheduled on Sunday at the Chapman-Moser Funeral Home. Family viewing hours were from two to four o'clock in the afternoon. Viewing hours were open to the public from seven to nine o'clock. There wasn't much to view as it was a closed casket. Greg's head trauma and bodily injuries were far too significant to allow for an open casket. His senior picture was framed and displayed atop his casket along with beautiful floral arrangements and casket sprays that had been sent by family, friends, and various members and businesses of the community. Silk banners with gold lettering adorned the arrangements with titles such as "son, brother, grandson, and nephew."

Dad went ahead to the viewing services to ensure that everything was in order. He needed that time alone with his son before the rest of the family arrived. The shock of seeing her son's casket was almost more than Mom could bear. As she was walking into the funeral home for the first time, she fell to her knees and began screaming and weeping. It wasn't easy for any of us. We were all taken aback by the presence of the casket before us. The sound of my mother screaming and weeping was horrific. Our immediate family was given time alone with Greg before the others could pay their respects and once we we were able to get Mom in some sort of condition to be able to receive family members. Family members from our large family started coming from all over the area and beyond to comfort and support my parents and pay their respects to my brother. Dad stood at the entrance to receive each person in line first. With a broken back, he was barely able to stand. Despite excruciating pain, he persevered. It was an issue of pride and respect for him. After talking with Dad at the entrance, attendees paused at the casket to honor Greg and then made their way to Mom who was sitting in a chair near the casket. She was barely able to lift her head. It was an emotionally and physically exhausting process. Mom, Dad, Jimmy, and I as well as various other close family members endured two emotionally grueling hours of receiving one grieving extended relative at a time, one embrace and condolence at a time. The lengthy process was followed by the grand finale as we attempted the harrowing task of removing Mom from her son's casket.

After all extended relatives had vacated the building, Mom laid across the wooden box that encased her son's body as she wept uncontrollably in unfathomable grief. The agonizing realization that she was leaving all that was left of the child she carried in her womb for nine months then gave birth to, raised, nurtured, and loved unconditionally for nineteen years consumed her mind, body, and soul. Dad was equally mourning the loss of his son, his namesake, who bore a striking resemblance to him, like his own reflection staring back at him in the mirror. He was the leader of our family. He had to be strong for Mom and for his remaining children who were also in unspeakable pain from the tragedy. As much as Dad attempted to remain strong in demeanor, I could see the tears that quietly rolled down his cheeks.

It stood out to me. I could only ever recall witnessing my dad crying a couple of times in my life. Once when his brother Gary was tragically killed in a motorcycle accident and another when him and Mom separated. I'm sure he cried on other occasions but he rarely ever showed "weakness" outwardly. He was raised at a time when they were taught from a young age that boys don't cry, especially not in public. Nobody expected that Dad should not be weak. He placed that responsibility upon himself. Under the circumstances, all ingredients were present to create a recipe for a nervous breakdown. Under that type of pressure, he had no choice but to escape to the privacy of the parking lot behind the funeral home at one point and screamed to the top of his lungs to release the pent-up pressure and pain.

Before any of us could come up for fresh air, the clock struck seven, and it was time to return for round two of the public viewing hours. As we neared the funeral home, there was an astonishing sight before us. There was a crowd gathered in front and around the entire perimeter of the building. Yellow school buses filled with high school students offloaded the buses. Reminiscent of Saturday football games, it seemed that the entire village and surrounding areas were in attendance. My family was humbled and comforted by the outpouring of love and support by the number of lives Greg touched. Close friends, classmates, football teammates, teachers, and coaches came to pay their respects, and were deeply affected upon viewing the casket, struggling to make sense of it all. Due to the amount of people in attendance, the allotted visiting time quickly passed by. The funeral director allowed an extension under the circumstances. However even then, not everyone was able to go through. In hindsight, it was likely a blessing in disguise. I'm not sure how much longer Mom, Dad, Jimmy, and I could cope with. After everyone left, it was nearly impossible to keep Mom away from the casket again. Somehow by the grace of God, we managed to remove her, administered her medication, and assisted her home to bed. After all, she would require rest for what was to come the following day.

It was a warm and sunny day that Monday morning May 2, 1994. Although the sun shone brightly when we awoke (not that we slept much), it was dark inside our hearts and our minds. Upon arriving at the funeral home, the setting very much resembled that of what it had been the night before as family, friends, and the community gathered for the ceremonialism of this tragedy. The service was scheduled to begin at ten in the morning. There were masses of people congregated around the premises and a line outside the building, which was also bordered by yellow school buses filled with Dolgeville High School students. Regardless of how creatively the funeral director and employees attempted to cram people inside the building, many were simply unable to get in without violating fire department regulations. Regardless, even those who were not able to enter the building remained for the services just the same, even if it meant being outside.

It was like most funerals, I suppose. Music played softly in the background during the opening prelude while funeral attendants escorted us to our seats. Rows of chairs were set up in the room where the funeral service would commence. Our immediate family was escorted to the front row, facing the podium where our childhood pastor would speak. Greg's closed casket was before us. There were candles lit on either side of the casket and beautiful floral arrangements and casket sprays adorning the casket. After everyone had taken their seats and the room was filled to maximum capacity, the service began with a formal introduction, words of welcome, opening prayer, and scripture reading. Pastor Martin took his place at the platform. He had been our childhood pastor at the Assembly of God church we attended growing up back on the Plant. He loved Greg and our entire family. He had relocated and was pastoring another church in Gowanda, near Buffalo, New York. However, when our family reached out to him, told him the tragic circumstances, and invited him to officiate the funeral, he agreed, grief-stricken. He made the four-hour trip to our small hometown.

The ceremony began. As Pastor Martin delivered a heart-wrenching and passionate eulogy, I looked around almost as if it was all transpiring before my eyes in slow motion. A mood of deep sorrow, confusion, despair, and hopelessness filled the air around me. The air around me felt saturated with grief. I felt like the oxygen was depleted, leaving me gasping for air. As the oxygen dissipated, my heart became poisoned with despair and despondency. The room was filled with familiar faces of family and friends. I glanced left and right and caught a glimpse of my mother, father, brother, grandparents, aunts, uncles, cousins, neighbors, and the entire school body as their faces were tear stained and their eyes swollen and bloodshot. The entire atmosphere was melancholic and the crowd was beaten and battered with grief.

After Pastor Martin's message, there was a pause for special musical selections. Greg's former girlfriend Julie compiled several songs of various significance on a CD and gave it to my dad when we had made funeral arrangements. One of three songs on it was Greg and Julie's special song. He absolutely loved the song and used to sing it to her whenever it came on the radio. There was a moment of silence as the song began to play. "Look into my eyes, you will see what you mean to me. Search your heart. Search your soul. And when you find me there, you'll search no more. You can't tell me, it's not worth fighting for. I can't help it, there's nothing I want more. You know it's true. Everything I do, I do it for you." As the love ballad played, it was almost more than any of us could bare. We were already barely able to contain our composure. The sound of weeping and sobbing nearly drowned the beat of the base and pitch of the treble as Bryan Adams' wailed out the lyrics of the love song Greg dedicated and often sang to the girl he wanted to marry one day. As if listening to that song was not emotional enough, the next two songs were no less touching. The songs "Power of Love" by Celine Dion and "Hero" by Mariah Carey created an atmosphere of deep sorrow as we all reflected on the tragedy.

After the musical tribute, Coach Walczak made his way to the podium to address the crowd and spoke accolades about my brother. Pastor Martin closed out the services with a closing prayer, and we were given instructions by the funeral director for the interment to follow. We were given an opportunity for a final viewing at the casket before the pallbearers were called forward to take the casket outside to the hearse. Beginning with the last row and working forward to the front row where my immediate family members were seated, we were led row by row from our seats to the casket. As with the two prior occasions, we struggled to pry Mom from the grip of her body enveloping the casket like a blanket. The pallbearers lined up outside of the door while each family member and attendee exited the building. The pallbearers were Jimmy and six of Greg's close friends: Gerald, Richie, Scott, Danny, Steve, and Jason. There were also two honorary pallbearers, our father and our cousin Kerry. Kerry was only nine years old at the time and unable to physically lift the large casket, but he was a male family member who was close to Greg and wanted to be included. Dad still had problems with his back at the time so despite his strong desire to carry his son, he was simply not physically able to. As an alternative, he was allowed to accompany the casket alongside the others as an honorary pallbearer.

Dressed in gray football T-shirts adorned with blue writing that bore my brother's name and number, the men were ushered into the funeral home by the funeral director. They lifted the heavy casket, which contained the body of our beloved Greg, and carried him to the hearse. With four men on each side and my cousin Kerry and dad in the back, they placed my brother's casket in the back of the hearse and the funeral director secured the door shut. Each pallbearer then made their way to the vehicle specifically reserved for the procession. The funeral attendants escorted my mom, Art, Harry, and I to the black sedan funeral vehicle that would follow directly behind the hearse. My dad and Jimmy rode in the car for the pallbearers. The procession was led by a black sedan that bore the white funeral flags with hazard lights flashing to make other motorists aware that a funeral motorcade was forthcoming.

Although I was nearly out of my right mind in that moment, I do recall that this particular funeral procession was one of the most overwhelming I had ever been a witness to. There were nearly one hundred vehicles, including three school buses lined up with headlights that could be seen from a distance of a mile away. It was by far the largest funeral procession I have ever personally been to, other than some notable funerals I've watched on the news. It seemed as if the ride from the funeral home to the cemetery was one of the longest fifteen-mile trips at a pace of 30–40 mph I have ever traveled. My mother barely lifted her head the entire ride as she wept on and off, very much medicated by sedatives prescribed by her general practitioner. Cold and damp, the sun peeked through the clouds occasionally. The lead funeral vehicle, the hearse, and the family sedan arrived at the cemetery deep in the North Country not far from our old home on North Road.

If you recollect a few chapters ago, I talked about the road that would come to bear great significance in this story. Never in a million years had anyone told me that I would one day embark on a journey down a road I traveled most of my life in a black funeral sedan following the hearse which carried the body of my little brother in it, would I have ever believed it to be true. You see it on movies and on TV, but you never anticipate living out some of your worst nightmares. The parade of vehicles and school buses followed the lead vehicles into the cemetery through the long dirt-and-gravel road that encircled the entire cemetery grounds. The pallbearers exited their vehicle and congregated behind the hearse. The funeral director got out and opened the door to the hearse. The pallbearers removed the casket from the back of the vehicle and carried it to the freshly dug, tent-covered grave. They placed the casket on a lowering device over the grave and proceeded to line up as an honor guard on the far side of the casket opposite the family.

Standing under that tent in the cold, damp air next to the grave that would soon swallow my precious brother, I was faced with the reality that this was indeed the beginning of the end. Witnessing the casket being lowered into the ground was more than any of us could bear. Weeping was the only sound that resonated in the atmosphere. Pastor Martin gave a brief graveside sermon and officially closed out the interment. At the conclusion of the service, all but immediate family members were dismissed after paying their final respects. Each pallbearer and immediate family member laid a rose on the casket as they said their final good-byes before the casket was lowered all the way into the grave. One by one, each pallbearer, cousin, aunt, uncle, and both sets of great-grandparents and grandparents approached the casket.

I watched each and every one bid their final farewell as they placed their rose on the casket, dreading my turn that was quickly approaching. I didn't want to say good-bye. I wasn't supposed to be saying it. Not like this! My grandparents went just before Jimmy and me. They were not young. They never could have possibly imagined outliving one of their precious grandchildren. Grandpa Daley had been my spiritual guide most of my life but even he didn't have answers for something like this. Grandma Foster placed her rose on the casket and began moaning and sobbing, "My Greggy! My Greggy!" as she fell to the ground. I feared I would lose my grandparents soon after this, which was very literally killing them softly.

The time had come. It was my turn to say good-bye to the little brother I loved so deeply. He had been my playmate, protector, and was one of my very best friends since we were young. How would I say good-bye? How was I going to carry on in life without him? It was so unfair! Why did this happen to our family? Hadn't we been through so much already? Our life was seemingly marked with greater amounts of suffering, affliction, and defeat than joy, success, or victory. Wasn't there more? Grandpa Daley said there would be a great reward one day for our perseverance in trials and tribulations. He said we would have a beautiful crown awaiting us at heaven's gate one day. Right now, I couldn't visualize the crown. Even if I could, I don't think it would have made a difference. I didn't want it anyway. It just wasn't worth the cost to receive it. It didn't feel like a gift in this moment. The only fixation in my view was intense pain. I slowly placed my rose on the casket and laid my head on it as if I was resting on my brother's chest as I said my final good-bye. My tears streamed down my face and spilled on the side of the casket. How could this be? I could not bear to part with him for a final time. I sealed my unconditional love for him with a kiss as I placed my lips against the cold, hard, and lifeless casket then stepped aside to make way for a far worse scene as my parents bid their final farewell to their beloved son.

I witnessed my mother and father say their final good-bye to their son when everyone had left before he was to be lowered into the earth, and it was horrifying. My mother screamed and wept uncontrollably. She placed her rose down and clung to the casket of her son she loved more than life itself. We allowed her the time she needed and eventually had no choice but to pull her away. We practically carried her to the car as it became increasingly difficult for her to stand against the weight of her own grief. The scene was equally heartbreaking as Dad parted from his son for a final time. I had never heard a man weep from the pit of his gut as I did that day. He shouted, wailed, and lamented. The heaviness in his heart was so overwhelming. His namesake, his mirror image, and his heartbeat was now gone. The will to live for a mother and father after losing their child must be extremely strong and amazing. Burying a child is something no parent should ever have to do. Children are supposed to bury their parents, not the other way around. Unfortunately, things don't always go the way we plan them. What is thought to be the natural progression of life sometimes takes a detour, and the order gets mixed up. It's impossible to imagine how to pick up the pieces or even think about taking another breath, knowing that you will never be able to hold your child again, kiss them, hug them, witness their smile, or wipe away their tears and tell them it's going to be okay.

As we pulled away, the funeral attendants lowered the casket into the grave and began shoveling dirt on top of the hole. Greg had returned to the ground from which he was taken. For dust he was, and to dust he would return.

15

Little Black Box

For there is nothing hidden that will not be disclosed, and nothing concealed that will not be known or brought out into the open.
—Luke 8:17 (NIV)

The days, weeks, and months that followed were much of the same. Our entire family was absolutely devastated, struggling to go on with life as usual. How do you go on when nothing is normal any longer? Life as we knew it had been shattered. We thought our family was ruined after the divorce and we were all living separate lives. Except now, one of our family members was gone forever. Our hearts still pumped blood through our arteries yet functioned as though they had flatlined. Very much going through the stages of grief, our minds were battered with great sadness, confusion, anger, denial, and despair. It was weeks before Mom or I returned to work and Jimmy resumed classes. Even then, it wasn't because we were functioning at full capacity. It was more a matter of survival, keeping our minds and weary souls occupied and as a means to socialize. Left alone and isolated with our grieving thoughts was a dangerous place to be. Dad did not even have that benefit as a viable option to him. He was still very much going through the pain and necessary medical treatments because of his back fracture.

As if the timing could not have been worse, I learned I was pregnant with my second child. It's not that I didn't desire to have more children. All I ever wanted in life since I was a small child myself was to be a wife and mother. However, I was not a wife yet and already a single mother. I was young, just under twenty-two years old, and had only been dating Harry for eight months when we learned we were expecting. We talked about marriage and children in the future. I had just hoped that this time, I would have a dream wedding first before having more children. There I went mixing the order up again. More so than that was the fact that I was barely surviving. I cried all the time, I was in therapy and prescribed antidepressants that could be harmful to a fetus, I couldn't eat anything without getting ill, and I was unable to get a full night's rest. How would I take care of myself at all, let alone tend to prenatal matters or even carry a pregnancy to term in the condition I was in. I later realized it was very much a gift and a blessing in disguise, which accomplished exactly the opposite of what I feared. Rather than allowing my emotional state of mind dictate the health of my unborn child and the result of my pregnancy, this child, the little girl I always wanted, was very much the gift God was providing as a means of subsistence. Even though, yet again, I had not done things according to God's intended design for my life, He was faithful to take my getting the cart in front of the horse and used it for my good and His glory.

Slowly but surely, I was recognizing that all that my grandfather had taught me about God since my youth was very much active and at work in my life. As a result, Harry and I started attending church. It was a journey of allowing Jesus to take the wheel in my life. Once I finally fully surrendered, I have never looked back, not because it's been easy, but because He is faithful and it is worth it. The little girl Harry and I welcomed into the world nine months later, naming her Brittany Rose, was a demonstration of God's grace and mercy in my life, even when I didn't deserve it. I had to force myself to stop crying, eat healthy, get enough sleep, take care of myself, and not self-medicate. She was a provision of the Lord in my life, even though I didn't deserve it, not because I am good, but because HE is good. He had a plan, a good plan, but I didn't recognize it then. I do now.

Jimmy also struggled to find a way to continue living without his big brother, his confidant, and his best friend just as I did. Greg's friends sort of took Jimmy under their wings. He was already close to them since he spent a great deal of time with them when Greg was alive. They all hung out together often. The group previously dabbled in drugs and alcohol before this tragedy occurred. Young, lost, and trying to find their way now that their entire worlds had been turned upside down by such a traumatizing loss, the group fully immersed themselves in a lifestyle of alcoholism and drug addiction. Self-medicating became a coping mechanism as they searched and longed for something—anything—to fill the void in their lives. Jimmy was only sixteen years old at the time, very much at an impressionable age, already attempting to figure out who he was in his adolescence. Now he was forced to figure out not only who he was as an adolescent, but also who he was without his big brother and best friend. Jake was only a toddler. He had just turned two years old. Greg loved Jake and was very much active in his life when Dad had Jake over for a scheduled visit. Although Jake noticed that Greg wasn't around anymore, thankfully he was a bit young to fully understand all of the details. He did, however, sense the loss of the big brother who wrestled with him and gave him horseback rides. While immediate family members and those who were extremely close to Greg just barely existed in the aftermath of his tragic death, acquaintances and others who knew him more casually moved on. Life must go on, business must return to business as usual, the school had to finish out the school year, and the community had to continue functioning.

That is where the rubber very much meets the road. In the initial phases of the tragedy, people banned together and supported those most affected with a showering of love and care. However, not long after the funeral service was over, society moved on. Before the grass has begun to grow over the grave, life all around us very much continues forward. While those left behind in the aftermath remain stuck in a nightmare of reality, looking out a lens of shattered glass, at everyone else who is seemingly happy and whole.

Those who move on certainly mean no harm. It's just how the world continues rotating on its axis. It's the natural order, progression, and design of the blueprints contained in the masterplan. Folks try to remain sensitive to the fact that although they very much see a physical appearance, essentially, you aren't really there. A shell with merely a heartbeat and blood flowing through your cardiovascular system, survivors lack cognitive ability to think, feel, or function normally. Left in a mind-set of merely existing, those who care attempt to console with a word of encouragement, sympathy card, a prepared meal, and financial or memorial contributions. Our little hometown really did make great effort in tending to those types of details and random acts of kindness. For instance, our local school retired number twenty-five football jersey in honor of Greg. No member of the Dolgeville Blue Devils football team would ever represent the number twenty-five again. Ms. Shapiro, Greg's art class teacher, left his desk exactly as it was for a long time. Our family wasn't aware of that until years later when she sent an email to my mom regarding graduation awards in Greg's honor and mentioned something that seemed rather insignificant to her at the time, yet it spoke volumes to the family he left behind. The graduation commencement six weeks later, which Greg would have otherwise been a part of, went forth. Awards were given to the graduating senior football player who performed effectively under pressure and to the graduating senior who showed the most technical improvement in his or her artwork in memory of Gregory A. Foster Jr. A brick was also placed in front of the school with Greg's name on it along with others who passed away. A picture of Greg in his football uniform is displayed in Brix, a popular Italian restaurant owned by a very good childhood friend of Greg's named Teddy, in our hometown to this day. His life and death clearly made a lasting impact that reached far beyond family.

A couple of weeks after Greg died, mom received a package in the mail. It was a red hardcover book. A letter was enclosed with the book. The letter was written by the publisher and stated:

Dear Family,

>*As publisher of the enclosed volume entitled Come Unto Me, we have been instructed by a number of your local community leaders to send you this inspirational memorial in this your time of*

sorrow. It is their fervent hope that in the pages of this remembrance, you may find the comfort, conso- lation, and hope of the Christian message of eternal life. On behalf of the sponsors of Come Unto Me, we extend their deepest sympathy.

In the margin of the letter was a listing of three area businesses that purchased the book for our family in memory of Greg. They were the local supermarket, Licari's Big M Supermarkets; Forget Me Not Florist; and insurance agency, Hopson-Luther & Harper Inc. At the bottom of the front cover in gold lettering was imprinted, "In Memory of Gregroy A. Foster." That was exactly how it was printed, "Gregroy." Mom went to the local businesses to personally thank each of them and let them know how much it meant to our family. She pointed out to Mr. Licari, the owner of Big M, that Greg's name had been misspelled. He apologized and said that he would have it corrected. She responded, "No, I didn't tell you so that you would correct it! I love it just the way it is! My son was dyslexic so I feel like this was exactly how it was supposed to be!"

It was like honeycomb to her weary soul yet the taste of her grief was still so bitter. Mom spent the majority of her days at the cem- etery when she was not working. During her lunch hour and after she left work at the end of each day, she would go to the cemetery. The amount of time she spent each day at her son's graveside was unhealthy, yet she didn't know what else to do. Dad was much the same. He would wake up in the middle of the night and drive up the long, dark, and wooded road to the cemetery, which was only a few miles from his house. He would lie on the grass over Greg's grave. The grass seed scattered on the soil over Greg's coffin received plenty of water that year from Mom and Dad's tears. Dad spent countless hours at the track where his son lost his life, investigating and strug- gling to make sense of it all. After all, he really had not received any satisfactory answers to all the questions he had. Finding out what happened to his son and how he was killed became the purpose of his life. Mom never wanted to know the details. She was barely sur- viving each day not knowing exactly what happened. Knowing was more than she could bare. Dad dealt with his grief just the opposite way. He had to know. He was unsatisfied with the vague information we had received and how he was treated like a criminal rather than a grieving father by officials investigating the matter. Anger is one of the several stages of the grieving process, and Dad was very much experiencing that phase of mourning. However, more than just being a natural progression of the process, his anger was fueled by not receiving answers to the questions he so desperately wanted. There was so much that didn't make sense, explanations that didn't add up, and so much that almost seemed to be guarded.

There were only three eyewitnesses to the incident that took my brother's life. Three high school seniors, two girls and a boy, who were classmates and friends of Greg's since elementary school. The boy was my brother's lifelong friend. They had met as young children in Royal Rangers at the church we attended, went to school together, and were teammates on the football field. They weren't as close as they had been in previous years since they had a different set of friends. Greg took interest in skateboarding and became close with the group he skateboarded with. However, they still occasionally hung out together at parties and in school. Of course, the three teenagers were traumatized by what they had witnessed. That was certainly understandable and expected. There was so much that didn't necessarily make sense to Dad, and when he attempted to gain clarification, he was told by law enforcement that it was an active investigation, therefore details were privileged and could not be released to him even though it wasn't officially still being actively investigated. Dad attempted to contact the three peers with Greg that night. Dad was told that they didn't see what happened and that they were minors and did not have parental consent to speak about the incident or told that they had legal representation. He was to address any of his phone calls or questions to their attorneys. But why would innocent bystanders who were supposed to be my brother's friends need to have lawyers? Why would they not give my parents answers they certainly had every right to know? How did this tragedy happen, and why did their son lose his life?

The girls weren't talking at all, and the boy's statements were inconsistent. According to the information Dad received, the boy provided three separate accounts of what happened. Allegedly, first he said that Greg was on top of the bridge and fell as the train went through. Second, he reported that Greg was playing chicken with the train and couldn't get off on time because he either tripped over the track or his shoelace became caught in the track. Lastly, one extremely troubling account was that Greg stood in front of the train because he was committing suicide. Although the formal investigation ruled it as accidental, a rumor spread in our small hometown, which was somewhat prone to gossip, that my brother committed suicide. My family knew Greg was not suicidal. It just didn't make sense. The last time any of us saw him either earlier that day or the day before, he was in good spirits. His friends who had seen him earlier that day but were not with him at the time of the incident said he was in a pleasant mood. He was not filled with doom, gloom, hopelessness, or despair. In fact, he was hopeful about his future. He just had a conversation with our father the night before he was killed about moving back home that coming weekend and about the process for joining the roofer's union after graduation. He even went as far as to tell Dad that he was going to ask Julie to marry him. In fact, he had just spent the night with Julie the night prior to his death. A few weeks after his death, Mom received a telephone call from an air force recruiter who asked to speak with Greg. She informed him that he passed away. The recruiter was shocked to hear the news since Greg spoke to him about possibly following in Dad's footsteps and enlisting in the air force. My brother was clearly making plans for his future. Thus, unlike most instances when someone is suicidal, he was not depressed or hopeless. Also, one does not typically commit suicide in the presence of three friends as they are laughing, talking, partying, and enjoying their night. The set of circumstances just was not consistent with a suicide.

Even if it meant that he never really did learn exactly what happened in those final moments of his son's death, Dad needed to know for his own peace of mind that his son did not in fact take his own life. One question Dad struggled with was why the three peers left the scene. Why would they just leave his son, their friend and classmate, lying there in a pool of blood alongside a train track like roadkill. The engineer and conductor reported that when they ran back to the location of impact, the three people who were with my brother fled, and a passenger reported seeing at least one of them run off. Thank God the coroner determined that Greg died instantly upon impact. I can't bear to think of my precious brother lying there helpless, mangled, and alone with no one to stay by his side. To their credit, it was a gruesome scene. They were young, seventeen and eighteen years old. They had just experienced the most horrifying trauma of their lives. There were no cell phones back in 1994. There was no way to dial 911 at the scene or call for help. They later reported that they left in order to get help, which certainly made sense. However, why didn't at least one of them remain at the scene with their friend until they could get some emergency assistance? The three had clearly been traumatized, not only by nature of the tragedy and how gruesome the scene was, but also because someone they knew and cared about, their friend whom they had grown up with since childhood, was the victim. There was no denying that something as serious and traumatizing as this could certainly cause for lack of judgment in sound decision-making and for the details of what exactly happened to be foggy or even confused with other events and instances.

Dad knew that Mom, Jimmy, and I as well as others who were close to Greg could not handle knowing the details of what happened to Greg or that he suspected there was something we were not being told. So he went into protector mode and attempted to shelter any of us from knowing the details or that he was even searching for answers. Yet he needed to know for himself so that he could begin mourning the loss of his son and for his own peace and closure. Dad finally had no choice but to hire an attorney to get some answers. It took years but with the assistance of attorneys, he was able to obtain police reports, photographs, witness statements, the official testimonies of the engineer and conductor, and a transcription of what was recorded on the little black box of the train. Sadly, he came to regret all that he finally gained access to. The pictures of his broken and mangled son were a horrifying reminder of the last vision he had in his mind for years when he had to identify his son's body in the morgue that tragic night. For so long, he had searched for answers about how his son lost his life and no one would talk to him, no one would provide an explanation as to what they witnessed, and no one would release information. He knew that there had been several different stories rumored about what happened that tragic night on April 28, 1994. None of them added up or made sense. But he never imagined what was written in the eyewitness reports of the train engineer and conductor he now held in his hands.

April 28, 1994, 8:35 p.m., transcription of Amtrak Train number 289 black box recorder:

> *"What's that up there?" the engineer inquired.*
> *The conductor replied, "What's what?"*
> *"Don't you see those two guys up there? What are they doing?"*
> *"Yes, I see them now."*
> *The engineer sounded the horn. "Are they clear?" He sounded the horn again a second time. "Are they clear?"*
> *"I think so, but they're still very close."*
> *Traveling at a speed of over 100 mph, it was seconds before they first noticed the boys standing on the track until they were right up on them.*
> *"Oh my god! I hit them! Oh my god! I thought they were off! Oh my God!"*
> *The engineer let off the throttle and applied the emergency brake. At the speed they were traveling, never expecting anyone to be standing on the track, it took the silver bullet 1609.344 meters (the equivalent of one mile) down the track to come to a complete stop.*
> *"Did that kid push him?" the conductor asked in a panic.*
> *"I think so!"*
> *"I gotta call it in!"*

Their voices were not recorded on the black box after that point since they had both exited the train to go back to where the impact had occurred. However, included in the file of information that my dad received from his attorney were the official statements provided to the police and Amtrak by the engineer and conductor upon formal interviews. They radioed into their command center at Amtrak. "We've had an accident on the rail with two males. We have located one of the bodies. We are looking for the other one."

They reported their exact location then got flashlights and started looking for the second male. The emergency official relayed to the two men that first responders were being deployed to their location. The emergency operator asked if anyone else was at the scene, and the engineer stated that there were two other females at the time of the incident but that they were no longer there. By that point, the teens reached the police station. The police radioed down to the other emergency responders at the scene that all three of witnesses were at the police station and accounted for and that no others were involved in the incident. It was confirmed that a second person had not been hit and that they no longer needed to search for another body. The reports from police interviews of the train engineer and conductor were consistent with one another. They had been interviewed separately, but their accounts of the incident were the same. They both reported that the engineer saw two people when he rounded the corner on the tracks. They saw the pair put something on the track. We later learned that they had been dropping quarters on the track. When the train would pass through, the weight of the train would flatten the coins, and they were fascinated by it. The engineer and conductor saw both males get off the tracks. They were walking alongside the track toward the train. My brother, subject one, was on the right closest to the track, and subject two was on the left. Both were facing the oncoming train. They were horse playing as they walked alongside the track side by side. The engineer sounded the horn twice, once when he first noticed the two boys on the track and again a second time as he approached because they were still too close to the track and he wanted them to move away. As he approached, the two boys were still horse playing, and it appeared to them that subject one was pushed by subject two as the train approached. Subject two attempted to recover and pull subject one back but it was too late. There was an instantaneous collision with the train. The engineer and conductor heard two separate thumps as the train made contact twice. They thought that they had struck both boys. A female passenger reported that she saw one person run off through her passenger window. The conductor statement matched the engineer statement. Both men were placed on administrative leave pending investigation and had to undergo drug and alcohol testing. Both were cleared of any drugs or alcohol in their systems and cleared of any wrongdoing.

Of course, this new information changed everything for our father. He finally received his long-awaited answers, however, he was not prepared for them. What would he do now with the information he had? It had been years since the incident happened. The case was closed. People had moved on. He wasn't interested in digging anything back up or making anyone in our family relive the most tragic day in our lives. He wasn't even interested in causing trouble for those involved. At the end of the day, he wanted to believe in his heart that there was no foul play involved. This was just an occurrence between two teenage boys horsing around where they shouldn't have been, and what was intended to be innocent fun turned into tragic circumstances. We were all suffering the cost, including those with him. After all, this was a friend. They had known each other most of their lives. Since they were just little boys, they had attended church functions together, gone fishing, built forts, went to school, played football, and partied together. Now they experienced the unimaginable together. There was no denying that this was a terrible and tragic accident that had traumatized those who witnessed the incident and all of the family and friends Greg left behind.

Dad didn't know what to do. He was angry but he was not sure of how to proceed so many years later after the case was closed. Nearly ten years later, the boy started reaching out to dad. He called multiple times and left messages. Dad did not call him back. His girlfriend at the time (now wife) encouraged Dad to call the boy back to get the closure he needed. After all, he had contained this secret in the prison of his own heart for so long. His soul was poisoned with anger, bitterness, and unforgiveness. Dad finally returned his call, and the two decided to meet at a nearby convenient store where there was a seating area available. As the boy, now a grown man, began to tell Dad that he wanted to talk to him about what happened that tragic night so many years ago, Dad became emotional. He was angry, hurt, and heartbroken all at the same time. He said indignantly, "I know what happened. Why did you lie to me?" The boy did not have a response. He just broke down in tears and left. They have never again spoken.

As I began my own investigation in preparation for telling this story, I reached out to each person who was with my brother during his final moments. One of the girls responded, but she continued to deny that she saw or knew anything that happened. The boy, now a grown man, responded and we had a long conversation late one Sunday night over social media messenger. The following is his account of what happened on April 28, 1994. He said that this was his first time ever sharing this story with anyone.

I've dissected that day, literally, thousands of times. So many times, I wished I tried to tackle him or wrestle him off the tracks. Either I would have saved him or died with him. But never in a million years would I have thought he was going to do what he did.

About five minutes after the first train went through, we heard another train whistle. I pulled change out of my pocket and laid it on the tracks like Greg did. We could hear the train in the distance but couldn't see it. We all backed up away from the tracks. We were standing about fifteen feet from the set of tracks closest to us. The train was coming on the far set of tracks. There's a slight bend in the tracks before the trestle so you couldn't see the train for a while after you heard it. As soon as the train came into view, Greg ran up to the tracks. We thought he was messing around and would get right back off, but he didn't. He raised his arms, fists clenched, and started screaming. We started yelling at him to get down, but he just kept screaming. I remember the train hitting the trestle, and I started running toward him. I looked to the left, and the train was on top of us. In a split second, it went from the trestle to us. It was a passenger train and moving twice as fast as the first train. I let out one last scream, and Greg turned and tried to dodge the train to his left. The only thing I can think of is he misjudged the speed of the train. He almost made it out of the way but it hit him. There was a sickening thud that seemed to echo in my ears for days. He flew right past me, spinning like the blades of a helicopter. He landed on the side of the closest track to us. His head hit the track really hard.

We sprinted toward him. I stood over him, expecting his head to be bleeding but didn't see any blood. I was checking out his head when one of the girls said, "He's dead!" I looked down, and she was taking his pulse. Again, she declared he was dead.

I screamed to go get help. The girl that was driving said we need to get to Dolgeville and get an ambulance. I told her that Little Falls is closer. I knew the fire department, ambulances, and police were all in the same spot. But the girls were screaming that we needed to go to Dolgeville for some reason. They started running to the car. I had no idea what they were going to do so I turned and ran after them. I remember thinking how far away the car was. He was thrown so far from where we were. Running up to him I didn't realize how far it was. I was screaming that we should go to Little Falls, but they said they didn't know where it was. We were all in tears it was complete chaos. I froze, literally par-

alyzed with fear, not knowing what to do. I didn't want to leave him since I didn't know what they were going to do. In my head, I was telling them where the police station was, but the next thing I knew, they were pulling me into the car.

The girl driving said, "I'm going to Dolgeville." I protested as it was too far and started directing them to the Little Falls police station.

Just as we hit the city limits, one of the girls said, "Oh my god! There was so much blood!"

"Blood?" I asked. "I didn't see any blood. What blood?"

She said, "His foot was gone!"

I asked, "His foot?"

She said, "Yes, his foot was gone!"

I was so concerned with his head, I never saw his foot. Still, to this day, I don't know what foot it was, and I don't want to know. I said, "If that's the case, we should have put a tourniquet on it."

She started crying uncontrollably that she didn't think of a tourniquet. We pulled up to the police station and ran inside. There was a lady at the counter. We started screaming that our friend had been hit by a train and told her where. She told us to sit down and sent an officer on the way. We heard him over the radio. He was having trouble finding the road. We could hear his radio communications when he found Greg and used his belt as a tourniquet. The ambulance made it in but got stuck coming back out. The officer had to push it out with his car. They took him to little falls hospital, and you know the rest.

*****

It's now twenty-three years later, and that's all we have. The engineer's and conductor's reports and an account from one eye witness with Greg at the time he was taken from us. They are two clearly different accounts of what happened. I don't know if we will ever truly know what happened that spring night, not on this side of eternity anyway. Beyond what exactly happened that night, our bigger question all of these years has been, where is he now? Dad essentially kept what he learned all those years ago locked in the prison of his own heart and mind. He has shared it with very few people. I don't know if what he found out gave him the closure he desired. In fact, it's quite possible he will never have full peace and closure, not on this earth. I believe he desires an honest conversation, acknowledgment, or apology. It would be the respectable and noble thing to do. Forgiveness and release can come even without acknowledgment or an apology for a perceived pain. It surely can't come in our own human capacity or strength. Forgiving the unforgivable even when it hasn't been requested by the one needing forgiveness is essentially a process of allowing God to do in the supernatural what we cannot do in the natural. Even if we must repeat the words "I forgive you" to ourselves all day long every single day, over time, the poison and power of unforgiveness eventually loses its potency in our hearts, minds, and souls until hopefully, we mean it when we speak the words.

How did the rest of us move on? Well, it took time, a very long time. They say time is a gift and even heals wounds. I would have to agree to an extent, but some wounds never truly heal. They may stop bleeding and close yet a scar remains. With time, it fades but it's always there. Some days, depending on what we wear or the temperature outside, it shows up more than other occasions. Still it remains. Life must go on. Mom and Dad chose to keep living when nothing inside of them wanted to live anymore. They kept going for the children they still had and very much needed them. Dad has since re-married Dianne and has gained a daughter-in-law, a son-in-law, eleven beautiful grandchildren, a great-grandchild, and multiple stepchildren and step grandchildren. He still lives in Upstate New York in the same town we grew up in. Mom is remarried to Art. She has gained a daughter-in-law, a son-in-law, a stepson, ten grandchildren, and one great-grandchild. She eventually relocated to Virginia and has resided there for over the past twenty years.

We sometimes wonder what Greg's life would be like today if he was still alive. He had much of his future planned since he was supposed to be graduating and had begun mapping out his future. Would he have married Julie like he planned to? Would they have children? Would he have joined the Roofer's Union like Dad? Would he have remained in the hometown he loved and planted roots of his own here? As for Jimmy, Jake, and I, we all eventually got married. Jimmy has been married to Laura for sixteen years and they have six children (Noah, Adah, Nathan, Elsie, Samuel, and Benjamin). Harry and I have been married for twenty-two years and have four children (Zachary, Brittany, Belle, and Lola Grace). Our daughter Brittany just had her first child two years ago, which made us grandparents to Luke Gregory (my brother Greg's namesake). Jake enlisted in the army and is stationed in Texas. He recently welcomed his first child into the world, Cole Gregory, also named after our brother. Jimmy and I also eventually moved away. We both relocated and traveled quite a bit but primarily lived down south and planted roots in Virginia for about twenty years. We have since both moved back to our hometown in Upstate New York. There's a very good reason for our decision to do so. This story has quite a bit to do with it, but we'll get to that shortly.

It's difficult to sum up all that's transpired in each of our lives over the past twenty-three years since Greg left us. It is undeniable that Greg's life and tragic death has very much impacted each of our journeys in profound ways.

I will say that God promises to take what was meant for evil and work it for good. That thing—or in my case, several different big life trials—the devil meant to take me out, God used for my good and His own glory. In fact, as I reflect upon the lives of my immediate family, extended family members, and even some of our friends, this tragedy has been that thing that the devil meant to take us out. Instead, God used it for good. Just like Grandpa Daley always said as he often quoted Grandma Daley's favorite Bible verse, "And we know that in all things God works for the good of those who love him, who have been called according to his purpose" (Rom. 8:28 (NIV).

16

The Note

Jesus answered him, "Truly I tell you, today
you will be with me in paradise."
—Luke 23:43 (NIV)

As I mentioned in previous chapters, I surrendered my life to the Lord when I was sixteen years old at a youth conference in Boston, Massachusetts. However, I was young, immature, and in a relationship with a guy who had a different religious background than I did. He did not support or understand my decision so my submission fell on poor soil and did not take root or bear fruit in my life. However, after the tragic loss of my brother and several other life-devastating circumstances the Lord used to allow me to hit a place of rock bottom, I recommitted my life fully to Him. As God was working all things for good in my life, he was simultaneously actively pursuing my brother Jimmy as well. Like my story, the Lord used Greg's death to radically save and transform Jimmy's life as well, and he surrendered his life to Christ in December 1997.

On June 1, 2013, after my brother Jimmy's transformational encounter with God, his eventual journey led him to his ultimate purpose and calling on his life, to share his story with the world as an evangelist. After a dozen or so years of planting roots in Virginia, Jimmy responded to the calling on his life and obeyed the Lord. As a result, he packed up his wife and children and relocated back to our hometown in Upstate New York. Moving from down south to Upstate New York was not an easy decision for their family. His wife Laura was a southern belle. She was born and raised in North Carolina. She and Jimmy had moved just a little further north to Virginia shortly after they tied the knot but still very much south of the border. Leaving her family and southern roots was not a decision that came lightly. She was extremely close to her family, namely her mom. Leaving her mother to relocate twelve hours away was not an easy choice. It was equally difficult for Jimmy. Mom and her husband Art and Harry and I lived in Virginia. Jimmy had flourished in his walk with the Lord there. Leaving solid Christian relationships formed with mentors who very much took the young married couple under their wings was especially hard.

On the other hand, moving back home to Upstate New York was essentially returning to a place of very difficult memories and demons from the past as well as relationships and temptations that could lead him astray. Nonetheless, they trusted the Lord and obeyed His call on their lives to take a leap of faith and quickly began an outreach ministry for the lost and broken. About a year later, Harry, our three daughters, and I moved back home as well to partner alongside my brother in ministry. My son Zachary stayed behind to be with his girlfriend and establish a life for himself. Several weeks after transplanting to New York, my mother-in-law, who lived down the road from my brother's new home in the country, stopped by to speak with them. She offered to come along and help them in any way possible, mainly with child care assistance. In addition to having four children under the age of seven years old, Laura was pregnant with their fifth child. She was homeschooling the older children and very much appreciated any help available to her with the move. Barb, my mother-in-law, insisted that there was a man who needed to speak with Jimmy from Pine Crest Bible College, which was a nearby seminary. Jimmy didn't understand the importance of a meeting with him, but Barb was persistent. She approached Jimmy on several other occasions as she visited their home and inquired about whether or not he had been in touch with the man who wanted to meet with him.

One day, as Jimmy was checking his mail at the local post office, Barb pulled in the parking lot. When she saw Jimmy, she handed him a note on a little white piece of paper and said, "This is the man who wants to meet with you." The note contained two simple words, the man's name, Pablo Molina, and his telephone number. Jimmy did what any other millennial does in this day and age, he searched for the man on social media. After a successful search, he sent him a friend request. Shortly thereafter, Pablo accepted Jimmy's friend request, and the two began a short dialogue through instant messenger. They arranged a meeting the following evening at six thirty at the Pine Crest Bible College cafeteria.

It was Saturday, June 22, 2013. Pablo began to share a story with Jimmy of an encounter he had many years ago. It was April 1994 when Pablo turned over the key to the fifteen-passenger seminary van and drove into town. Pablo was responding to the voice of God as he pulled out of the campus parking lot and traveled about fifteen minutes to the local pizzeria and arcade in the Village of Dolgeville. It was at the Pizza Lab that Pablo would minister the gospel of Jesus Christ each Saturday night. His heart was heavy for the youth who wandered away from the Lord in this small municipality. Pablo loved God and the adolescents who resided in this small rural town. As he walked into the small pizzeria, he received many glares from the troubled teens he wanted to share the good news with that night. As Pablo sat down, many of the teens drifted to the back of the restaurant toward the arcade to stay as far away from the preacher as possible. This was not the first time they had seen this foreign-looking man who was originally from Bolivia. They knew why he was there. He came there often, and they did not embrace it. Pablo sensed their unwelcoming hearts but knew that God called him to this little restaurant to bring hope to the lost and broken. Pablo approached the counter and ordered pizzas. He hoped to share a slice or two with any teen open to chatting with him over a meal. He believed that God would unlock a door to their hearts and an opportunity to minister to them. Although he was often rejected, mocked, or made fun of for his beliefs, God would occasionally provide an open door for Pablo to share the gospel with a few of the adolescents who frequented the local hangout spot. He even had the chance to pray with some of these kids at times. He knew that his work was not in vain, although the rejection was certainly not easy. Still he remained faithful to the calling God set before him. The kids that he prayed for came from troubled or broken homes, many struggled with drug and alcohol addictions, some were exposed to physical and mental abuse, and a few had lost parents or siblings to death. For the most part, they were all good kids with high hopes for the future, but like lost sheep had gone astray, wandered from God, and were utterly lost.

On this weekend night, Pablo sat down at the booth that would ultimately become his pulpit for the next two hours. He looked up and saw one of two brothers who frequently taunted him the most. He suspected that they could possibly be twins but wasn't sure because one appeared to be slightly older than the other. Pablo didn't know their names. The two teenage brothers frequented the hot spot regularly. The older-looking brother stood at the counter in his long, black trench coat that he wore regularly. He waited intently for the owner of the Pizza Lab to exchange his dollar bill for four quarters to play arcade games in the back of the establishment. As he walked passed Pablo's table, a strong odor of alcohol trailed behind him as he hurried back to the game room, avoiding direct eye contact. Pablo was drawn to this boy he often crossed paths with at the pizzeria. God had highlighted this young man to the evangelist. Maybe because on some level, Pablo could relate. Perhaps there was an even greater significance. However, Pablo sensed an urgency and direct prompting of the Holy Spirit.

Although Pablo did not know what was going on in this teen boy's life or heart, he recognized a mirror-like image of himself at that age. Pablo observed this one lost sheep handing the four quarters to the younger brother, who deposited two quarters into the change slot of the pool table. Pablo had heard rumors that the brothers liked to drink and were well-known for fighting. As a matter of fact, the front of the Pizza Lab had become their fighting venue on Saturday nights. They would drink, smoke marijuana, and occasionally use hard drugs while waiting for their opponent. Once their adversary arrived, the juvenile delinquents would encircle the combatants in full display on Main Street in this small, otherwise quiet community. Frequently, the local police intervened, separated the rivals, and sent them home. However, this night would be different. The purpose for the Bolivian missionary being there at the Pizza Lab on this ordinary Saturday night would be fulfilled at the sovereign hand of God. The only battle that would take place at the property on this night would be the absolute war waged in all of heaven over one young man's soul. This particular night would not end in a customary way as the police would not be called to intercede. This was to be a celebratory moment when all the angels would rejoice over the one sinner who would turn to the Lord. As the neon open sign turned off at the close of business, the group of high school kids moved toward the front entrance of the building. Some went home, many would roam the streets of town, and several would assemble on various back roads and other isolated locations where they would party, drink, use drugs, or participate in sexual activities.

Pablo cleaned up his table and prepared to go home to the theological campus. He noticed the older brother picking up the cue sticks in the backroom. Pablo made eye contact with him and struck up a conversation. As they made their way to the front door, the young man in the black trench coat followed suit, proceeded down the front stairs with a friend in front of Pablo, and crossed the street. The faithful servant of the Lord followed the young man as a small crowd of teens lingered in front of the Pizza Lab making plans. Pablo knew his mission was clear in that moment. He seized an opportunity the Lord provided to pursue the lost soul and dig deeper into this young man's life.

"You remind me of myself when I was about your age," Pablo said to the teen boy. Somehow the Lord used those words to spark interest and curiosity in his despondent and nomadic spirit. Although this man with broken English was a foreigner on American soil, the universal language of the gospel message he spoke about was not foreign to this boy. It was familiar. He had heard this good news before as a child. His grandfather often taught him biblical principles growing up. He had a foundation. As a child, he attended Sunday school, Vacation Bible School, Royal Rangers, and even briefly, a youth group. Pablo added, "I was in your place at one time. We all need God."

To Pablo's amazement, this young man hiding behind the facade of his dark clothes that reflected the condition of his heart, listened attentively to the message the minister carried on his tongue like succulent nectar to a famished soul. Often before when Pablo tried to engage with this young man, the boy continued walking passed, ignoring and sometimes even snickering at the evangelist. The fact that he had even given Pablo the time of day was a miracle in itself. Perhaps Pablo could just plant a seed. As the crowd of teenagers on the sidewalk outside the pizzeria dispersed, some mocked and interrogated the boy, "Come on, what are you doing? Why are you wasting your time talking to that guy?"

However, unlike any other encounter, the boy seemed disinterested in the opinions of his friends and more interested in speaking further with this man about his struggles. The young man began to open up to Pablo, sharing his heart and the conflict within his soul that he inwardly desired to live right and do well. He didn't know how to successfully get out of the bondage that entangled him.

Pablo shared the hope of salvation and shared the good news of the gospel message with him. He assured him that there was promise in the transformational power of receiving Jesus as his personal Lord and Savior. Pablo explained that he could be a new creation in Christ if he believed and that there was a way out of sin and bondage. The *old man's* anger, hurt, and pain could die so the *new man* could be resurrected. The young man wanted to be new, wanted hope and a future, and wanted to be forgiven and cleansed from the bondage that enslaved him. The picture from heaven was beautiful as Pablo led this young man to the Lord. Pablo explained, "For God so loved the world that He gave His only begotten Son, that whoever believes in Him should not perish but have everlasting life" (Jn. 3:16). He assured the boy that God had a wonderful plan for his life! "I have come that they may have life, and that they may have it more abundantly" (Jn. 10:10). He explained that to be made whole or be saved is to submit to God and his plan and purpose for our lives. It is a turning from our old ways and turning to Jesus, to ask him for forgiveness from our sins, and to give us new life in Him. Pablo said, "To receive Christ as your Savior, you must first admit that you are a sinner and need to be saved. Second, you must repent and be willing to turn away from your sin. Third, you must believe that Jesus Christ died for you on the cross. Fourth, you must receive Jesus Christ into your heart and life."

Pablo walked the boy through what is commonly referred to as the Roman's Road.

1. "For all have sinned, and fall short of the glory of God" (Rom. 3:23).
2. "For the wages of sin is death; but the gift of God is eternal life through Jesus Christ our Lord" (Rom. 6:23).
3. "But God demonstrates His own love toward us, in that while we were still sinners, Christ died for us" (Rom. 5:8).
4. "That if you confess with your mouth Jesus as Lord, and believe in your heart that God raised Him from the dead, you will be saved" (Rom. 10:9).
5. "For whosoever shall call upon the name of the Lord shall be saved" (Rom. 10:13).

Pablo invited the young man to pray with him. He agreed. Pablo instructed him to repeat after him, "Lord Jesus, I know that I am a sinner. I believe you died for me on the cross so that I might be saved. Right now, I ask you to forgive me of all my sins. I open my heart to you. Come into my heart, Lord Jesus." The angels in heaven rejoiced as they welcomed the soul of this sinner into the holy of holies. The Spirit of God was awakened in this brawler's life. After the boy repeated the scripture and the words soaked in, he whispered, "Amen."

Heaven erupted with singing and praise! He had been given a new birthday! He was new! He was saved! He was a part of the holy family of the King! He entered the Pizza Lab that Saturday night lost and left with a new destination. His eternity was secure, having liter- ally turned around and went home a new man in Christ. Pablo was elated about the opportunity the Lord ordained that night. He excitedly returned to his van with a bounce in his step and heart pounding, thrilled about the miracle God had just performed. He was jovial as he drove back home, having won a soul for the Lord and claiming back what the locusts had stolen. But the truth is, Pablo didn't fully understand the significance of this moment. He didn't fully understand how God would use this moment to impact a person, a family, an entire community, and reaching far beyond.

One week later on April 30, 1994, Pablo returned to the Pizza Lab as he did every Saturday evening. Many of the usual group of teens were there that night. There were some missing. Specifically, Pablo looked for the young man in a long black coat he led to the Lord the previous Saturday night. He never did ask his name the week before when he spoke with him. However, he was clearly the older teenage boy who always wore the black trench coat. The missionary didn't see him, which was unusual. He was regularly there on Saturday evenings. Pablo overheard some chatter amongst the group of teens who were in the eatery, and it seemed to be dialogue of a serious nature. The youth were talking about some sort of train accident, but Pablo only heard bits and pieces over the noise of many teenagers and restaurant patrons ordering food and arcade games in the background. He ordered pizza and wings as he always did on Saturday nights and asked some boys he had gotten to know and formed friendships with to join him as they usually did. When the boys sat down to share dinner with him, Pablo asked what train accident they had all been talking about. The teens began sharing with him that there had been an accident a few nights earlier. One of their friends was struck and killed by the train. They were visibly shaken up over it. Pablo mentioned that he had vaguely overheard something about the accident on the news but didn't know the details. It was revealed later that the one they were speaking of was, in fact, the older brother who wore the long, black trench coat he led to the Lord one week ago.

Pablo audibly gasped at the devastating news and became distraught in his spirit. He was unable to eat as he became physically ill with grief. He struggled to offer some encouragement to the boys who just lost a dear friend and traveled back home to share the news with his wife, Christy. They were both deeply saddened over the disparaging news they received that night but were comforted by the hope that God had mercy on this young man's soul and ordained a divine intervention just a few days before his fate had been predetermined. Very much reminiscent of what they recognized to be a thief on a cross type of testimony, they were amazed at the grace of a loving Father whose arms were not too short or mighty to save his precious son at the eleventh hour right on time. Pablo continued sharing the remainder of the story with Jimmy.

17

Wedding Day

He will wipe away every tear from their eyes, and
there will be no more death or mourning or crying or
pain, for the former things have passed away.
—Revelation 21:4 (BSB)

Pablo and his wife Christy, who was also present at the meeting that Saturday evening on June 22, 2013, continued sharing their story with Jimmy. Brief memories began to enter Jimmy's mind as they communicated with him. He was one of the teens who frequented the popular pizza establishment back in the 1990s. He began to vaguely recall a man who closely resembled this man now sitting across the table from him at the Bible college cafeteria. Yes, it was him. He remembered him. He never knew his name at the time so it didn't resonate until that present moment. As if this meeting and reminiscing were not all mind-boggling enough, there was still more. What did this have anything to do with Jimmy? Why did they want to speak with him? Why were they sharing this story with him?

As if a switch on a light bulb had been turned on, Jimmy had a pivotal moment in his thoughts. Could it be? This boy in the black trench coat – our brother Greg used to wear a long black trench coat. He also frequented the Pizza Lab. Was this young man in the story Pablo led to the Lord and later found out was tragically killed by a train Greg?

Pablo and Christy continued sharing their story. Pablo continued going to the Pizza Lab every Saturday night. Eventually, a colleague from the Bible college went with him. After a while, others would join them. It very much became an outreach of the ministry. Eventually, Pablo and Christy returned to their country of origin, Bolivia. Over the course of nearly twenty years, they traveled as missionaries. The Lord gradually led them back to the United States and back to the Bible college they went to many years ago. The name had been changed from Pine Crest Bible College to Bethany Bible College. They moved back on campus and very much became involved in the ministry again.

An event called Reign Fest was started in 2009 in our hometown of Dolgeville. Reign Fest was an all-day Christian rock concert started by an old classmate and friend of Jimmy's named Bobby. He had given his heart to the Lord in recent years as well and was prompted by God to organize a concert event that would serve the purpose of providing a child- and family-friendly music festival in our area. His desire was to demonstrate to the local youth that being a Christian doesn't equate to lack of fun or enjoyment. Jimmy and Bobby had contacted one another through social media and stayed in touch. Upon learning of Jimmy's radical life transformation, Bobby invited Jimmy to be a special guest speaker at that summer's upcoming Reign Fest.

After months of planning and preparations, the big day arrived. Hundreds of concertgoers from all over the region and beyond purchased tickets for this special occasion. Jimmy prepared a powerful message to share with the crowd that evening as the special guest speaker. He had just recently begun speaking and ministering at various churches and events. He was a powerful, vibrant speaker with an incredible message to share. The lineup for the evening was dynamic for this part of the region in the North Country. Christian recording artists Disciple, The Awakening, Silversyde, Isaiah Six, Everyday Sunday, Gracie Levendusky, and NF and special guest speaker Jimmy Foster were on the agenda for the event. The bands primed the hearts and minds of the concertgoers to hear an encouraging message from my brother. He began sharing his testimony. It was compelling. He imparted how God saved him and rescued him from the bondage of addiction. He had been enslaved to a spirit of rebellion against God. For years, he had been down a wayward path because of the traumatic effects of his older brother's death by an Amtrak train and self-medicated with drugs and alcohol. Jimmy shared how the tragedy impacted him and how the Lord used it to accomplish incredible good in his life for God's own glory.

Christy Molina was in the audience that night as Jimmy spoke. As he shared his remarkable testimony and provided the details of his brother's tragic death, something resonated with Christy. The Lord drew back to her mind the story of the young man in the long, black trench coat that her husband met many years ago. She could not wait to go home and share the news with her husband. This had to be the brother of the boy her husband had led to the Lord just days before his tragic death. They never knew his name or knew how to reach out to any member of his family. Quite frankly, they didn't know the family, didn't know how the information would be received, or if it was even appropriate to share. They certainly did not want to appear as though they were in any way attempting to play *heroes*, for lack of a better term. She returned home after the event had concluded and excitedly shared the news with her husband. She told Pablo that there was a guest speaker in town from Virginia who spoke about his brother who was tragically killed there by an Amtrak train in 1994. She told Pablo that she believed this speaker was the brother of the young man he encountered in the Pizza Lab who wore the black trench coat.

Pablo agreed that it had to be him. He asked her if she spoke to the guest speaker. She responded that she didn't really know what to do or if he was in fact the brother so she wanted to consult with him first. However, Jimmy returned to Virginia the very next day, and they had no contact information for him. God wasn't finished yet though. He had a plan. He began stirring in Jimmy's heart after the Reign Fest experience. God placed a burden on Jimmy's heart for his hometown and for his friends who still lived there. He and his wife began to pray about the situation. One year later almost to the date in June 2013, Jimmy, Laura and their children left Virginia and relocated to Upstate New York.

As I mentioned in the previous chapter, my mother-in-law Barb lived just down the road from my brother and his family. She babysat for the children often. She was retired but worked part-time at Dolgeville Central School as a bus monitor. One day, Barb was speaking to a woman she worked with who was a bus driver about babysitting for her daughter-in-law's nieces and nephews. As they spoke further, her colleague began to make an association. The family Barb was babysitting for was the family her very close friends, Pablo and Christy Molina, talked about at Pine Crest Bible College. Dawn the bus driver had been involved in the ministry many years ago and remembered Pablo and Christy sharing this story with various members of the church. Dawn told Barb the story of the boy her friend prayed with before he was killed by a train. Barb affirmed that her daughter-in-law's brother was killed by a train. Upon making a determination that the family Barb was babysitting for was indeed the family of the boy Pablo shared the gospel with nineteen years earlier, Dawn handed Barb a note. She wrote Pablo's name and phone number on a piece of paper and requested that Barb pass the note along to Jimmy for him to call Pablo. The next couple of times Barb babysat for my nieces and nephews, she told Jimmy there was a man who wanted to meet him. However, Jimmy didn't know the man and could not imagine why he would have desired a meeting so it wasn't an immediate priority to get in touch with Pablo. His wife was pregnant with their fifth child, and they were amid getting unpacked and settled in with four children at the time. He was also traveling quite a bit for work. Several weeks later when Jimmy stopped by the local post office to check his mail, Barb happened to be there as well. She asked him if he had contacted the man who wanted to talk to him yet. She was persistent in the assignment entrusted to her by her coworker to have these two men meet.

"Well, anyway, that's me, as you know by now. I am Pablo Molina and I wanted you and your family to know about the encounter I had with your brother nineteen years ago. The Lord opened a door for me to share the gospel with him days before he passed away, and he received the gift of salvation. He was saved."

Jimmy was overwhelmed with emotion. For years, our family yearned to know that God was merciful on Greg's soul. We knew that he had a similar experience as a child in church, but he was on a wayward and rebellious path. Lacking a distinct and visible demonstration of an inner working of the Lord in his heart, reflected by outward lifestyle choices in his final days, we hoped for the best. We had no choice but to trust in the character of the Lord. However, we were not absolutely sure of salvation or a knowing beyond the shadow of a doubt that he was indeed in heaven and that we would one day be reunited with him in eternity. Jimmy thanked Pablo and Christy for sharing this glorious news with him and told them that he would share it with his parents and siblings. He called our mom and dad, as well as Jake and me the next day to share the news. We were all shocked, overwhelmed, elated, and relieved to know that after nineteen long years, we had reassurance that our beloved Greg was spending eternity in heaven and that we would one day be reunited with him again.

After I hung up the phone with Jimmy, I was overwhelmed with emotions. There was such a tremendous joy and an incredible sense of profound relief. For nearly twenty years, I had agonized over my brother's eternal fate. It was horrific enough grieving his loss. The fact that it was such an unfathomable and gruesome tragedy compounded my anguish. The thought that my brother would endure eternal torment left me out of my mind at times in despair. Over the years, I talked to many therapists and even pastors about this very topic. All tried to provide me with some sort of comfort and peace, but deep within my heart, I wrestled with uncertainty. A former elder at the church we attended as children offered consolation that Greg had responded to an invitation to receive Christ as a child. Yet he was so far from the Lord at the time of his death, we never really knew for sure if he fully surrendered his life to Jesus. At least, that's how it seemed. Little did we know the inner conflict waging within his soul in his final days on earth. After I hung up the phone with Jimmy, I sat on my bed and reflected, attempting to absorb the answers to questions I had wrestled with my entire adult life. I mulled over my last interaction with Greg nineteen years ago. Suddenly, it all made sense.

The last time I saw or spoke with my brother Greg was a day or two before he left us. Something was different about his countenance and demeanor. He didn't seem depressed or angry. There was an indescribable joy in his overall presence. He was in a pleasant mood and seemed at peace. I noticed it at the time but hadn't really ruminated it until this moment. He seemed anxious to tell me about something. He talked to me about a lot of more serious things and when he needed advice. Of course, I was running late for a previous engagement so we agreed to talk later, but that opportunity never came for us. Was he planning to disclose his experience with me? He knew I would understand it. It was no secret that I had a similar experience at a church-related youth conference a few years prior at that time. Although I wasn't necessarily walking firmly with the Lord at the time, Greg knew I attended church. Oh, how I regretted not making time for him in that final moment even if only to tell him I loved him one last time. The bonus would have been possibly learning something that could have spared our family so many questions all those years. I wondered if he had ever had an opportunity to share it with anyone else before he died. Nobody had ever mentioned it to anyone in our family, that is, until recently in June 2017.

As I began researching, investigating, and interviewing friends and family for information I needed for this manuscript, I reached out to the boy, now a grown man, who accompanied my brother in his very final moments at the track that fatal night. The following is his account of what occurred just before the tragedy on April 28, 1994. These specific details further corroborate and confirm Pablo's testimony that it was indeed my brother Greg he prayed with days before his unexpected death.

April 28, 1994, approximately 8:00 p.m.

We were hanging out at the track, having a few beers, listening to music, and placing coins on the track. While we were there, Greg kept going back behind the car we parked nearby. I was curious about why he continued loitering behind the vehi-

cle. So I followed him at one point to see what he was doing. I caught him emptying his beer cans. I asked him why he was dumping out his beer. He said that he didn't feel like drinking anymore. I questioned him about his disinterest in drinking since it was unusual for him. He mentioned that he had spoken with a pastor at the Pizza Lab recently and was thinking about going back to church and getting his life straightened out. He seemed a little embarrassed about it. He didn't want the girls we were with to know he wasn't drinking. He just wanted to hold his beer can and make it appear that he was still drinking. He was secretive about his encounter with the man he presumed was a pastor. I think he was afraid of being made fun of, but we had attended church together when we were younger so maybe he assumed I understood it and wouldn't think he had lost his mind. Still, he didn't want anyone else to know. So I kept his secret between us that night.

It was not long after that unusual interaction between friends that Greg's fate was determined. In retrospect, knowing what I know now, I have a new perspective about that old track that I associated with tragedy for twenty-three long years. As I peek into the window of tragedy through the shattered glass of unfathomable loss and indescribable grief with eternal perspective, I am welcomed with an epiphany of sorts. Henceforth, as I have shifted my perception of the track, that represented so much calamity, I have been permitted a miniscule glimpse of heaven. I am reminded of Jesus' crucifixion when the two thieves crucified beside Him (Lk. 23:33–43) began mocking and blaspheming Him, as did many of the spectators. Jesus responded with the words, "Father, forgive them, for they do not know what they are doing" (Lk. 23:34). "Father, forgive them" is a prayer of unmatched mercy and love. Even in His agony, Jesus' concern was for the forgiveness of those who antagonized Him. It is important to note that Jesus' prayer does not mean that everyone was forgiven, unilaterally without repentance and faith. It does mean that Jesus was willing to forgive them. In fact, forgiveness was the reason He was on the cross. Jesus' words show the merciful heart of God.

The other thief rejected Jesus. While being tortured on the cross, he chose to join his persecutors in insulting the Savior of the world, most likely because he wanted the oppressors to think he was just like them and had no love for God (Matt. 27:44). Not only was this man next to the Savior, he heard Him pray, he witnessed the salvation of the other thief, he saw the world go dark, and he heard the testimony of the Son, but his pride kept him from submitting to the only One who could save him. Jesus' prayer to forgive them was answered in the lives of many people. Upon seeing how Jesus died, the Roman centurion at the foot of the cross exclaimed, "Surely this man was the Son of God!" (Mk. 15:39). One of the thieves responded in faith to the message of salvation and was taken to paradise that very day. He is the one usually referred to as the thief on the cross. A member of the Sanhedrin publicly aligned himself with Jesus (Jn. 19:39). A little over a month later, three thousand people in Jerusalem were saved on the day of Pentecost as the church began (Acts 2:41). While the other man did not respond in faith and is now suffering from a fatal mistake. It is remarkable that in the excruciating and mind-numbing torment of the cross, the Son of Man had the heart, mind, and will to pray for others. Yet it is a miracle that one thief, while in agony himself, heard the Spirit of God call him to repentance and salvation that God provided through the death of Christ. While the disciples were abandoning the Lord, this man answered the call, and his sins were forgiven, including his blasphemy against the Son of God (Lk. 5:31–32; 12:8–10). As a result, when the earth shook and tragedy became triumph on the most famous day in history, Jesus promised the thief on the cross next to him, "I tell you the truth, today you will be with me in paradise" (Lk. 23:43). What we learn from the saved thief on the cross is that we are all sinners in need of a Savior. No matter the weight of our sins, what we or the world think, or if our sins are minor or extreme, it is never too late to repent and accept the free gift of salvation (Eph. 2:8–9; Rev. 22:17). Moreover, as long as someone still has a mind and the will to choose life over death (Heb.

9:27), it is not too late to proclaim the gospel, which hopefully will open a heart to a miracle by the Holy Spirit.

Reminiscent to this story, I am reminded of the miracle of my brother Greg's very own "thief on a cross" story. Greg was known for mocking and harassing Pablo when he faithfully pursued the call of God. Greg didn't know in that moment of submission to the inner working of the Holy Spirit in his heart that his eternal fate was changed in that moment, which came to bear great significance just days later. God knew in advance that this was Greg's predetermined destiny. God didn't cause the horrific tragedy of my brother's death. However, for reasons we will never fully understand on this side of eternity, He allowed it. God pursued Greg but did not force Greg to receive Him. God isn't interested in prisoners and hostages. He gave him a choice. By the grace and mercy of a faithful, loving father, Greg accepted the free gift of salvation that cold April night. The outcome of the track would not be diverted that night. However, where my brother would spend eternity would change. What the devil meant for destruction in Greg's journey that had led him to that track, God turned into triumph. Greg's name was written in the Lamb's book of life and his place in Heaven was reserved.

As the headlights of train number 289 approached, in the twinkling of an eye, tragedy and triumph collided. There was a stirring in the throne room as all creation held its breath and Brother made the journey to his final destination. He arrived at the holy of holies. Dressed in white, Jesus welcomed his son home. I can't help but imagine Brother standing before his bridegroom, worn and weary yet dressed in white. He was whole. He no longer suffered the fragmented pieces of his body he left behind on that track as he wept in awestruck wonder, standing before the only One who could make it possible. Then with hands that bore the only scars in heaven, Jesus touched Brother's face and wiped away the last tears he would ever cry. He spoke the life-giving words Brother longed to hear, "Welcome home, son. I love you." April 28, 1994 no longer represented loss and tragedy. Love had come and finally set him free. April 28, 1994 was Brother's wedding day. Hand in hand, they danced in golden castles while inaugurating a beautiful exchange as Brother took on his bridegroom's righteousness. Then the clouds rolled back as Jesus took Greg's hand and walked him through the gates.

Our tragic loss was his eternal reward. We occasionally encounter him even though heaven and earth separate us. I haven't physically seen him since our last conversation, but there have definitely been occurrences when I have sensed his presence with me. I'm sure others in our family have experienced similar circumstances. Dad has certainly been aware of his son's presence at times throughout the years. Mom has had four specific encounters with her son since he left us. They have materialized through dreams. Recently, my mother had a brief encounter with Greg. He was dressed in a baseball uniform. As she helped him straighten his belt, he said eight simple words, *Crash it, receive it, believe it, and live it.* She repeated back the words he said, "Crash it, receive it, believe it, and live it." When she woke up, she continued repeating the words. She wrote them down so that she would not forget exactly what he said. She told me about the dream the next day and asked me to discern its meaning. I have thought and prayed a lot about it since that day. I didn't entirely understand its meaning or what it pertained to, but I felt very strongly that it was a message he wanted shared with the world through this narrative of his life. The Lord has given me some revelation and now I share it with you. It was always meant to be shared.

In the phrase, *Crash it, receive it, believe it, and live it,* there was a very clear and concise message and directive. I believe Greg's instruction for all of those he ever crossed paths with and the world at large was to crash through the walls and barriers people have guarding their hearts and minds. I believe that he specifically used the word *crash* to imply a sense of urgency. Don't wait another day. Today is the day that the Lord has made. Tomorrow is not promised. Had my brother delayed, his eternity may have looked very different.

"Receive it, believe it, and live it" is the simple message of the gospel. It's not complicated. Simply *receive* the gift of salvation, just as he did. *Believe it.* Don't waste time with doubt. *Live it.* Let your light shine in the world and be an example to all those watching your life on display. I believe that Greg appeared to Mom in a baseball uniform rather than a football uniform, the sport he most loved and excelled in, for a distinct purpose. In the game of football, winning is based on touchdowns. However, on the baseball field, the goal of the game is to make it back to home base. Likewise, I believe he would want to encourage anyone reading the words on these pages to know that in the end, the object of the game of life is to return home. I close with this visual. When I began my own journey on this track from tragedy to triumph, my mom sent me a picture of my brother Greg. He was about four years old, dressed in his favorite "gweem" and "wed" striped shirt he often wore. It was a picture my parents had taken of him at Santa's Workshop, the family attraction in the far northern part of Upstate New York with rides and animals. In the picture, Greg was kneeling down and embracing a lamb. There was a deeper meaning for me as I looked at the photograph, captivated in wonder.

Having been on this journey and learning all the Lord has revealed to me throughout it, I can't help but shift my focus and set my gaze on things above. As I look to the sky, I see the clouds through my brother's eyes. As an artist, he was always fascinated with clouds. He often described beautiful images and scenes he recognized in the clouds. Just a couple of weeks before his death, he was riding in a vehicle with our cousins, Trina and Sundi Rose. "Do you see that stairway to heaven up in the sky?" Greg asked Trina.

She responded, "No, I don't."

He insisted that it was there. He told my father about it when he returned home later that evening. He played the popular Led Zeppelin song, "Stairway to Heaven," on his drum set often. My dad attributed Greg's sighting of the stairway reaching heaven to the love he had of the song he listened to repeatedly and the manner in which he frequently described the clouds.

I sometimes find myself gazing at the sky as I sit on my balcony overlooking the Manhattan skyline. If I peer through the lens of eternal perspective every now and then, the Lord allows me to catch a glimpse of heaven. I can visualize the track where my brother lost his life, but it no longer represents tragedy. I wonder if the track was a stairway to heaven of sorts. When I imagine the top of the stairway, I see Brother. He looks happy and at peace, smiling and waving as if to say, "Sissy, look at me!" It's a breathtaking scene as he's kneeling down and embracing *the* Lamb who was slain for his own behalf. I can't help but wonder if he has the most exquisite drum set comprehendible, crafted in solid gold that glimmers all across paradise as he leads worship with the saints around the throne. There's a prophetic word with every strike of his foot against the bass of the drum. It's powerful enough to stir the heartbeat of every being he left behind as the beat of the bass intercedes and commands name after name into the Lamb's book of life. And sometimes, I ponder if every once in a while, maybe, just maybe, he twirls his golden drumsticks and beats out the drum intro of that song, well… you know…

The End

Notes

1. Lyrics used in Chapter 9: Singer/Songwriter: Bryan Adams, Producers: Bryan Adams, Michael Kamen and Robert John "Mutt" Lange, "Everything I Do, I Do It For You."

    © 1991 Robin Hood: Prince of Thieves Soundtrack and © 1991 Waking Up The Neighbours

2. Inspiration for Chapter 17: Casting Crowns, "Wedding Day."

    © 2011 Come To The Well Album, Beach Street and Reunion Records.

Acknowledgements

When the Lord initially gave me the phrase, "From Tragedy To Triumph," in the summer of 2013, shortly after a vision transforming phone call with my brother Jimmy, I knew it was supposed to be the title for a book I was being called to write. However, what I didn't know was what exactly it was all supposed to look like. I scribbled and jotted down occasional notes in various random spiral notebooks and on sticky notes laying around our home and even in the notes of my iPhone. Yet, I lacked clear direction. Until the Winter of 2016, shortly after watching an inspirational movie on a date night with my husband. Quite honestly, I had no idea what the movie was about, and the title did not interest me. However, I love date nights with my husband and I enjoy going to the movies. God had a plan. From that movie, I was inspired in a way I hadn't been in a very long time and several days or so later, that inspiration gave conceptualization to the story God called me to share with the world.

In an instant it seemed, writer's block was removed, and murky vision became crystal clear. The Track: A Journey From Tragedy to Triumph was birthed. There was one small problem. I felt as if I was being led to tell the story from the perspective of a non-fiction narrative or novel. Which was not what I originally envisioned several years prior when a stirring began within me to write what I imagined would resemble more that of a Christian spiritual growth book. I had absolutely no idea how to write a non-fiction novel. I don't believe I had ever even read a non-fiction novel in it's entirety before, let alone written one. Perhaps I did. I have a history of reading about half way through a book and then starting another. If by some strange coincidence I did read an entire novel from front to back in my lifetime, it would have likely been fiction and from the Little House on The

Prairie collection. Otherwise, a visitor in my home would most likely find predominantly Christian Life/Spiritual Growth books on various bookshelves, coffee tables, and nightstands.

So, I did what I suspect any other inexperienced writer would do and went to the local bookstore, found a non-fiction novel that seemed interesting, purchased it and went home and began reading. It only took a few chapters to begin to get a feel for what it may look like and so I did the only thing I could do at that point – grabbed my laptop and started pecking away at the keyboard. I managed to write the entire first chapter. I emailed it to my dad, who had been helping me gather the information I needed to write the story, so that seemed like a safe place to send my first stab in the dark. He responded, "Can I call you?"

We talked on the phone and he asked me if I wanted his honest feedback and was open to constructive criticism. Which essentially told me in the insecurity of my own heart that it wasn't good and there was absolutely no way any legitimate publisher would ever publish my writing. That isn't what he said though. He simply told me that it was very good and very well written. However, there was one recognizable problem. I had given away the entire plot of the story in the very first chapter of the book. He suggested that I create a bit of mystery and not share the plot right away, as in the first three pages of the entire book and that I come up with a different method to my madness.

So, after working through my feelings and insecurities, I went back at it again and gave it another shot. I sent the new and improved draft of Chapter one to him with simply one word in the subject line of the email, "Better?" He provided a resounding affirmation and the rest is history. I pray that this labor of love and seeds sown in pain and watered with tears will produce a great harvest in the very souls God intended this story for.

To my husband Harry, (aka Hun); you are my absolute best friend, soulmate and biggest fan. Thank you for believing in me, especially on the days I don't believe in myself (which are many) and for encouraging me to finally make this dream a reality after years of mulling it over. Thank you for your sacrifice of time over the past year as I focused on this project and for all the days and weeks you took over with the kids and released me to go back home for entire weeks so that I could get alone with myself and God to hammer out the words on these pages. Thank you for letting me cry on your shoulder on the hard days and helping me catch my breath when the pain of delving into the absolute worst hours of my life overwhelmed my soul. Thank you for every detail, including listening to every word on every page of this narrative as I read it aloud to you. I am eternally grateful for every facet you covered throughout the process, such as keeping the ship afloat financially to release me for a season to focus on a calling on my life and for every investment you made into this project to make it happen, trusting God to provide when I wasn't so sure. I love you.

To my children, Zachary, Brittany, Belle, Lola Grace, and grandson Luke Gregory; thank you for sacrificing your mama's (and for Luke – your Grammy's) time and attention at various points over the past year in order to release me to not only pursue a dream I have held captive in my heart for many years, but also allowing me to be obedient to God and walk into a calling He placed on my life for such a time as this. To the "A Team" (aka the two oldest), thank you for every phone call that didn't happen because you knew I was in my writer's groove and sacrifice when you genuinely needed mom from a distance. To the "B Team" (aka the two youngest), thank you for taking care of dad in my absence, and for essentially homeschooling yourselves independently, going to dad with Math problems, agreeing to allow dad to take you to auditions and events and for all of the days and weeks you subjected yourselves to dad's "cooking" when I was away for extended periods of time researching and writing. Which reminds me that I probably need to thank Papa Johns. $10 large, three topping pizza specials and rewards points for free dessert, not to mention delivery to our NYC apartment door no less than once, on a good week, twice on an extra special heavy writing week, kept my family fed for the past year and freed my hands to type rather than cook and do dishes. To my little Lukie, thank you for being my ray of sunshine on the cloudy days and never-ending supply of kisses, hugs and allowing Grammy to rock you when only the unconditional love of a baby could put a dent in the intensity of looking back. You will never begin to know the tears that were cried over you as you slept in my arms in the rocker glider in your nursery. I love you all immensely and everything I do, essentially is to leave a legacy for each of you.

To my dad, how do I adequately thank a man who went in deep to the absolute darkest hours of his entire life to give me the details I needed to write an accurate and effective story. For every late-night phone call and text message, (we're talking in the thousands here), thank you. For every time I called and said, "I don't think I can finish this," and you said, "Yes, you can," thank you. For your sacrifice in visiting "THE Track" with me as we very literally re-enacted the things so intense that they re-trigger trauma and PTSD, thank you. None of this would be possible without those details. I pray that in turn, the finished product provides you with a sense of closure and peace, as much as a father can achieve closure and peace in a situation like this. I hope you find your purpose in the pain as you read the words on every page. In the end, I hope that you are pleased with the finished product and proud of me. I love you.

To my mother, it's difficult to even write that statement, (to my mother). As a mother myself, I've come to appreciate just how much strength and courage you really have. I thought I knew, but I had no idea. How does a mother survive the unimaginable? I don't know that there is a good answer to that question. You have. For that, you are my hero. Someone once told me that those who have been through the absolute worst life has to offer have the most beautiful crowns awaiting them in Heaven. If that is true, and I believe that it is, yours is beyond comprehension mom. You earned each and every jewel it possesses. And if I know you like I think I do, I have no doubt whatsoever, that when you receive it one day and hear, "Well done, well done, thy good and faithful servant," the giver in you will lay it at the feet of the One who sustained you all of these years. Thank you for agreeing to go through the process when everything inside of you could hardly bare it, for answering all my questions and going through countless photographs that were difficult to reflect on so that a few could make it into the pages of this book. I know this wasn't easy for you and I am eternally grateful that you did it anyway. I love you.

To my brother Jimmy, thank you for also being willing to go backwards to an incredibly painful season of your life to advance the gospel. I know you get it when we count the cost for the Kingdom. Thank you for answering hard questions. Thank you for sharing with me the information that is contained in Chapter 15. Without it, this book is just tragedy minus the triumph part and without triumph, there is no purpose in our pain, no testimony of God's work and grace in our lives. Thank you for your sacrifice of love in uprooting and relocating your family to a place we called home for most of our lives and re-living many memories that aren't always easy for the advancement of the Kingdom. It matters. I know Greg is proud. I am too. I love you.

To our youngest brother, Jake, you were just a baby back in 1994 and by God's grace, you were spared from much of this, although even as a wee one, I know you sensed the loss and the grief in every family member around you. Sometimes I look at you and see something in your eyes or an expression that is so familiar and it makes my heart smile even for a moment. Thank you for your little notes of encouragement along the way. It truly meant more than you realize. I love you.

To my mother-in-law Barb, thank you for all your support throughout this journey and for filling in the gaps with Harry and the kids at times in my absence. Most of all, thank you for your faithfulness in passing along "The Note." Without your persistence, our family may not have ever had our deepest question answered. Within the pages of this book, I pray that your own questions about God and why bad things happen are answered. I love you.

To the rest of my husband's family, thank you for accepting this hot mess into your family and being my extended family for the past twenty-five years. Thank you for your support and encouragement on this book project. I love you all.

My list is getting long, and I have a very large family and most contributed something to this story. There are nearly a dozen first aunts and uncles, not including spouses, and well over thirty first cousins within the immediate branches of our family tree; certainly, too many to write a paragraph about each of you in this forum. However, you know who you are and what you each contributed to the story. I pray it brings a smile to your faces when you see a few of your names sprinkled throughout the pages. Thank you all. I love you all.

One Aunt that I need to recognize is my Aunt Me Me. I won't expand because I will make you cry and I've done enough of that over the past year. I couldn't not say thank you however, for allowing me to "interview" you about the excruciating details of "that night," and for answering the hard questions that I just couldn't bring myself to ask of my parents, for photographs, newspaper clippings and a never-ending supply of Grandma's iced tea on your front porch. I love you.

To all my BFF's, and I am not even going to begin to list them in this forum because I will inevitably leave someone out and hurt feelings and you all mean too much to me to ever allow that on my watch. You know who you are. Thank you for every late-night phone call, text message, Facebook message, mani/pedi date, lunch date, for conveying that you were inspired through watching my journey and sending me funny memes when I needed to laugh through the tears on heavy days. You are each a means of God's grace in my life.

To Julie…thank you for being the love of Greg's life. Thank you for revisiting the most painful memories of your existence. Thank you for sharing your love story with me and for allowing me to share it with the world. May it be your contribution to what the Lord is going to accomplish through your young love story and help you find purpose in your pain contained in these pages, healing for your soul and connection to a love story between you and the Savior, who has been drawing you all along. I wish you could see you through my lens. It's beautiful. I love you.

To Covenant Books and every member of the team who took my knowing nothing about how to write a non-fiction novel and helped me create something beautiful, your labor is not it vain and nothing short of a miracle. Taking something I pecked out on a key-board and creating a professional quality book was no easy feat. You are amazing. To Ladonna Giessman, my Acquisitions Agent, thank you for taking a chance on this small-town girl and believing in my dream and making it possible to take a dream and convert it into reality. Without a Publisher, The Track was merely a word document. To Ashley Matthews, my Publication's Assistant, thank you for your patience with my Type A, perfectionistic personality and answering every question with kindness and grace.

Last, but most certainly not least (this is definitely a saving the best for last concept), to Jesus Christ, my Lord and Savior, thank you for saving me! Thank you for loving me more than I love myself, for believing in me when I don't even believe in myself. Thank you for blessing me with a gift and then for giving me a story to write and entrusting it to me. I wouldn't have chosen it if it were up to me, but I am grateful that I'm not the one in charge and that you know what I need. Thank you that in all the darkest moments in my life, you have been faithful to me and have never given up on me. I will never understand this glorious grace. You rescue and save me daily, not only from trouble and death, but more importantly, from myself. You truly are my best friend and I am honored to share our relationship with the world and I pray that I have portrayed it in such a way that anyone who reads about it will desire it for themselves. I love you.

Finally, to every reader, every social media follower, to all those who have commented notes of support, encouragement and love, thank you. I would have absolutely quit every time it was too hard to push through the pain, were it not for the pressure to not let you all down. To every hurting and grieving heart, wrestling to understand and make sense of all that just doesn't make sense in this world, I pray that in these pages you find some of the answers you are looking for. I believe that within this story, every reader will take away something unique to your specific journey called life. It's been an honor to have you take the time to read about mine. I know there are a million other things to spend your limited time and money on. Thank you for making the choice to invest some of it here. I pray that in return, your individual stories will never be the same.

About the Author

Photo: April Kennedy

Jennifer Fox is a Certified Biblical Counselor, Certified Professional Life Coach, Author and Speaker. She counts it a great honor and joy to come alongside women in all walks of life and is equally passionate about marriage and family. She enjoys writing and sharing the stories God has given her through her own personal life experiences to give edification, encouragement, inspiration, and hope to the brokenhearted. She speaks and teaches about the same topics she writes about at women's, marriage, and parenting conferences.

Jennifer attended Seminary in Richmond, Virginia, where she majored in theology and biblical doctrine and minored in urban and inner-city outreach. She received her Christian counseling certification from Light University School of Counseling and Psychology and her life coaching certification from the Life Coach Institute of Orange County.

She lives in New York with her husband Harry; four children, Zachary, Brittany, Belle, and Lola Grace, a grandson Luke; and the family dog Joy.